FiRE UP Your LIFE!

Living with Nothing to Prove, Nothing to Hide, and Nothing to Lose

Ken Davis

ZondervanPublishingHouse
Grand Rapids, Michigan

A Division of HarperCollins*Publishers*

*This book is dedicated to the men and women
who by their faith have demonstrated
the abundant life that God intended
for all of us—and to my wife, Diane,
who is one of those people.*

*Some of the names of the people in the stories
in this book have been changed,
as have some of the details of those stories.
In most cases, this was done to protect
the privacy of those involved.
In other cases, I remember the stories
but have forgotten the real names!*

Contents

Introduction

Dave Veerman, a vice president with the Livingstone Group in Chicago, was living at one time in Covington, Louisiana. He'd been training hard for a marathon that would be run across one of the world's longest bridges, which spans Lake Pontchartrain. When race day came, Dave thought he was in pretty good shape—but a strong wind blowing directly in the face of the runners put his endurance to the test.

Fifteen miles into the twenty-six-mile race, Dave was exhausted. Every part of his body hurt. His morale was very low—and it got lower when women pushing baby carriages began passing him as though he were standing still. He felt as if he'd had a blowout in both tennis shoes, but he stumbled on. Every step was a major effort. Dave lost track of time and distance until finally he began to hear the cheers of the crowd at the finish line. He knew he was close.

Then he saw his wife and family. His wife was standing out in the road with a camcorder, recording his big finish. "Suddenly," Dave said, "I felt that rush of adrenaline. After all, I couldn't let my family see me finishing weakly. With about a hundred yards to go, I straightened up, shrugged off my exhaustion, and sprinted the rest of the way to the finish line!"

After Dave had rested, he and his family sat down at home to watch the video. Dave watched himself stagger into view, looking like a dying man dragging himself across the desert. He saw himself look up, saw that brief glint that shone in his eye as he realized that his picture was being taken—and then he saw himself continue on toward the finish line with the same shuffling gait, looking like an old man making his way to the bathroom in a pair of loose slippers at midnight! Although Dave had thought that he was sprinting to the finish line, in reality nothing had changed.

I laughed till I was sick when Dave told me that story. But every day that same scene is played out, with an infinite number of variations, in the lives of millions of men and women—and in life it's not so funny. The world is full of men and women who want all the excitement and joy that life has to offer. They've been running the race of life for years, but they feel tired and frustrated, trapped in bodies and hearts that will no longer respond. Occasionally they stumble across some motivation, perhaps a possession or position that they think will finally allow them to sprint again—only to discover later that nothing has changed. They *want* to run, they *try* to run, for a day or two they even *think* they're running, but in reality they're still stumbling in the terrible slow motion of a bad dream. Time is passing them by.

It isn't supposed to be this way. Even though it is difficult, the race that God has set before us was meant to be run with joy and excitement. But something happened along the way.

Ken and Barbara (no, not Ken and Barbie) are vivacious and involved. Their lovely-but-not-ostentatious home is the center of entertainment and fellowship for the people in their church. Looking at them, you'd tend to describe them as the ultimate couple living the ultimate life. But in a small-group Bible study, both confess that something's missing. One night Ken asked the group a question that stimulated discussion for weeks: "How do you get the most out of life?"

Ken asked the right question. It's one of the most important questions in life. And millions of people are asking it.

In response, I prepared and delivered a message entitled "You Only Go Around Once!" In that message, I was trying to help men and women recover some of the gusto that God intended for their lives. I was amazed at the response. That message touched people's lives like no other I had ever delivered. Many who were deeply dissatisfied with the quality of their lives found hope in the simple truths I shared.

But there's a problem with being used by God to deliver a life-changing message. While I was delivering it, I had to listen to it, too. It's not a comfortable thing to be convicted by the truth you're presenting to other people. I've spent much of my life trying to prove, with achievement and recognition, my worth—trying to hold at bay the gnawing belief that I really wasn't worth much. I was forced to acknowledge hidden doubts, sins, and fears. I became aware that I had been clinging desperately to the security of *things*—things that I didn't want to lose, despite my own deep sense that I was missing life's full potential.

Faced with these undeniable truths about myself, I began to apply my own message to my own life. I had been telling others that the Bible teaches us to live with *nothing to prove, nothing to hide,* and *nothing to lose.* Learning to live as if I really believed that to be true opened my eyes to the wonderful grace of God— a grace that frees me from the bondage of proving my worth, from the shame of hiding my sins, and from the futility of holding on to what will eventually turn to dust.

Applying those simple biblical principles revolutionized my life. Yes, I still have a long way to go. But God has used these principles to move me in a direction of fulfillment and purpose I have never known before—and from which I will never retreat.

You won't find a gospel of health and wealth here. I can't promise you giddy happiness, easy living, or great material success. And what good would it do you if I could? There are millions of people who have all of those things and yet live shallow, unfulfilled lives, just as there are millions of others who have none of those things and yet live vital, purposeful, enviable lives.

That, I believe, is the result that most of us really want for our lives. We want to live life to its fullest, our lives and attitudes in stark and beautiful contrast to the mundane norm. People who live life with gusto aren't limited to any one social or economic group. You can find these vibrant souls in all stations of life. Some live in the ghetto, and others live in corporate towers. Some are teenagers, and others are in the twilight years of life.

But all have one thing in common: they walk in intimate friendship with a God who is the source of their self-esteem, who is the loving forgiver of their transgressions, and who is their ultimate hope for security. They're living lives of fire. They have nothing to prove, nothing to hide, and nothing to lose.

Perhaps you're saying to yourself, *I'm really pretty satisfied with life. I'm not sure this book will be of any benefit to me.* Take a moment to answer the following questions:

Do you sometimes question your self-worth?

Do you wonder if your contribution to life is of any value?

Do you base your self-esteem on performance or physical appearance?

Are you easily affected by the circumstances around you?

Do you compare yourself to others?

Do you hide your true feelings?

Do you pretend to be something you're not?

Do you want to live a simpler life, but feel thwarted by society's demands?

Do you feel as if you're on a treadmill and desperately want to find a way off?

Do you cling to *things* that lost importance and meaning long ago?

Are you afraid to take risks?

Are you seeking adventure in illicit relationships?

Do you wonder why life doesn't have more to offer?

Are you often motivated by fear?

Do you cling to the safety of familiar relationships?

Do you try to impress those around you with evidence of your worth?

Have you lost your zest for living?

Are you tempted to spend more time in a fantasy world rather than face reality?

Are your decisions and actions governed by what people might think?

Have you turned to drugs or alcohol to cope with life?
Do you feel that your creativity is gone?
Have you lost your excitement about tomorrow?

If you answered yes to any of those questions, you could be clinging to energy-sapping attitudes that will keep you from living with the power and potential that God intended. If you answered yes to several of them, then I urge you to read on—you'll definitely find help in these pages.

I showed that list of questions to a psychologist friend, who read it and then asked, "Is this really a good test? I'm sure that *most* people would answer yes to many of these questions." Then, after a thoughtful pause, he added, "Of course, it's also true that most people are living far short of their potential. Most are not experiencing abundant life—and they know it!"

He was right. Most of us waste enormous amounts of time trying to manufacture fulfillment from achievement, recognition, material wealth, and a host of other sources that can't bring the satisfaction we desire. But wait—if our lives are so futile, so unfulfilling, why do we exert so much energy in the pursuit of something we've not yet experienced? What makes us think that fulfillment and meaning are even possible? The truth is that we share a common thread of hope—hope that life has more to offer than we are presently experiencing. I believe that God gave each of us that hope; and that's why, in this book, I have drawn heavily from the book that offers the ultimate hope for living: the Bible.

Because we live in a fallen world, life will always have disappointment and pain. Perfection will come only when God restores us to the glory he first intended for us. But for the person living with nothing to prove, nothing to hide, and nothing to lose, even the disappointments of life become a part of an exciting challenge.

What difference has this kind of living made in my life? It has freed me from the control of circumstances. It makes me want to get up every morning and take full advantage of the possibilities for that day. It frees me from the bondage of trying to measure up to society's idea of success.

The personal productivity that results from this kind of living can't be measured by titles, social recognition, or bank accounts. Instead it is measured in the unrestricted joy of the heart. Living with nothing to prove, nothing to hide, and nothing to lose will change your life explosively and allow you to touch and change other's lives for the better, too.

Sound good? Then welcome to *Fire Up Your Life!,* a book that offers hope to those who have lost hope, new possibilities to those who are bored with merely coasting—and *life* to some who feel that life is over.

Part 1

LIVING WITH NOTHING TO PROVE

Chapter 1

You Only Go Around Once!

It's funny how some television commercials stick with you for years. Who can forget diminutive Clara Peller peering over the fast-food counter and demanding, "Where's the beef?" The soulful rhythm of Ray Charles and the Raylettes singing, "You got the right one, baby—*uh huh*" pops into my mind every time I see a soft-drink can.

One commercial, even though it hasn't aired for years, still haunts me. The ad opened with a scene showing several young people sailing a catamaran. (A catamaran is a sailboat that looks like two canoes held together by a trampoline.) These breathless, athletic kids had set their sail in such a way that the boat skimmed through the waves precariously balanced on just one canoe. The smiles of the young people were only slightly distorted by the surf's spray on the camera lens, and their laughter provided the background for the authoritative voice: "You only go around once—so reach for all the gusto you can get!" The voice then suggested that drinking a can of beer would provide all of the gusto that life had to offer. The ad ended with a lusty challenge: "Go for the gusto!"

It was a powerful message. Thousands were motivated to buy the beer, subconsciously (or maybe even consciously) hoping it would bring gusto to their lives.

Sorry, beer drinkers. Gusto living doesn't come from drinking a can of beer any more than it comes from eating a slice of watermelon. I still remember the gusto one of my high school friends got from drinking a whole six-pack. He threw up until there was nothing left in his stomach. Then, crying for his mommy, he tried to throw up some more. But there was nothing left. He was so sick that I expected to see his tennis shoes come flying out.

Two days later, in the locker room, he boasted about the great time he'd had that night. Great time? Even as a teenager, I knew that was nonsense. If having painful dry heaves makes for a great time, why buy the beer? Just sneak off to a private place and stick your finger down your throat.

Still, I was fascinated with the issues this commercial raised. Advertising executives are intelligent people (for the most part) who intimately understand what motivates you and me. When they made the "Where's the beef?" commercial, they knew that millions of frustrated fast-food customers had stared at the thin wafer of "meat" set in front of them and silently wondered, "Where's the beef?" They created an ad that identified with that frustration and sold millions of hamburgers.

Advertisers also knew that because we had hundreds of available soft drinks to choose from, we were vulnerable to a catchy tune that identified the *right one, baby*. Clerks across the country hummed "uh huh" as their cash registers rang up record sales of Diet Pepsi.

The "gusto" beer commercial was especially effective, because it appealed to one of the most basic of human desires: to live life to its fullest. First, the ad softened the viewers by reminding us, "You only go around once." For those who have no hope of eternal life, the brevity of life and the certainty of death are particularly unpleasant thoughts. Many New Age philosophies and old-age heresies make desperate attempts to circumnavigate those simple truths, but such attempts are in vain. Despite the philosophical gymnastics and metaphysical magic, the truth remains. Shirley MacLaine isn't coming back as an Indian princess or as a sacred bird. She isn't even coming back as a brick. Just like the rest of us, she will only go around once.

The advertisers knew that a reminder of mortality would catch our attention, just as it has throughout history. This ploy is used effectively to sell life insurance and to encourage us to accumulate material things—to buy, buy, buy. As the old saying goes, "We have to make hay while the sun shines." But the advertisers also knew that it would spontaneously ignite the desire within us to make the most of this life. Now they had us where they wanted us: primed and ready for their "Go for the gusto" message.

Searching for Life in All the Wrong Places

Unfortunately, without an understanding of life's purpose and direction, the desire to go for the gusto can lead to some pretty misdirected paths. "You only go around once, so reach for all the gusto you can get," said the ad.

And silently the viewers asked, "How do I reach for the gusto?"

And loudly, persuasively the advertisers answered, "Just drink our beer." No reasonable person would accept that as a valid answer. But are the answers we substitute for it any more valid? The truth is, when we're reminded of our own mortality, we desperately try to fill the void with some kind of "beer": hectic activity, overachievement, material wealth, recognition, personal power, pleasure, and pseudo-adventure, to name a few. These diversions help us forget the shortness of life. They bring momentary excitement to a mundane existence. But in the end, they keep us from experiencing the real thing.

On the opposite end of the spectrum from those who try to find substitutes for fulfillment are those who have simply given up on life. They find their solace in a sea of apathy. "Who cares?" becomes their motto. They refuse to think; they refuse to be challenged. I have met many of these depressed, sad people. They remind me of wounded birds waiting for the inevitable end. In many ways, they have died already.

Interestingly, the "gusto" commercial appeals to both groups. Alcohol can create the illusion of adventure and excitement, or it can numb you to reality. Both extremes are a dead end. Both lead to bitterness and disappointment. Both settle for second best.

Jim had taken the apathy route. His attitude and personal appearance screamed, "I don't care!" The television set was his refuge, and his family was little more than an annoyance. At work, Jim did just enough to get by. Both his job and his marriage were in jeopardy. He had given up on life. Jim reminded me of an old movie: *Night of the Living Dead.* He was still walking around, still going through the motions. But he was dead.

An extreme case? Maybe. But there are variations of Jim everywhere. Most still care enough to keep up the outward appearance of life, but inside they are dying, waiting for life to do to them what it must.

Heather was on the opposite end of the spectrum. Whereas Jim acknowledged his hopeless view of life, Heather used activity to hide from hers. As she put it, "My life is one constant rush." If there was a new drug, she wanted to be among the first to experiment with it. She moved from relationship to relationship, staying only until the initial thrill wore off. Heather never missed a party, and her laugh could be heard wherever the action was.

I met Heather while I was working as a stand-up comedian. One night, after finishing a very late show, I found Heather weeping on the steps of the theater. Why? Because her plans for the evening had fallen through, and there was no place to go. She couldn't bear to face the evening alone. She begged me to take her someplace, anyplace. Even if I had, I couldn't have resolved the anguish she felt. That pain came from a much deeper place that only the love of God could reach.

Alcohol had made Heather just uninhibited enough, just open enough, that she allowed me a glimpse of her emptiness that night. We had a long conversation, but what I remember most were her last words: "Please don't leave me alone. When I'm alone and have nothing to do, then I have to think. I don't dare think, because I don't have any answers." Heather knew she could only go around once. She had clung to the same hope the rest of us cling to: that life promises more than we're experiencing. It hadn't taken her long to discover that parties and booze didn't hold the secret. But at least that hectic lifestyle allowed her to forget the emptiness. As long as she was partying, it didn't matter. Later, in the quiet moments, reality would come crashing in. Life seemed to offer so much more to other people. Why was she missing it?

There are thousands of Heathers crying quietly each day. Some are homemakers hiding in the fantasy of soap operas. Some are men and women with careers clawing their way to what they think is the top. Some are people rushing to volunteer for church work or for worthy community causes. Some are variations of Jim: they haven't given up yet, but they've decided to coast. All of them experience those moments of pain when they have to ask, "Is this all there is?"

Born to Be Mild?

God never intended that life be a continuous orgy of activity designed to block out the truth. Nor did he create us to be spiritual and social couch potatoes oblivious to the opportunities around us. God gave each of us a certain potential and then designed us to be at our most satisfied when we're living up to that potential. In one way, that beer commercial was right. God created us to live with gusto.

"But isn't it selfish and therefore sinful," I have heard some people argue, "to want to live an exciting, fulfilling life? What if God's will for you is to forget your own hopes and aspirations and live a life of rather boring service to others?" Nonsense! Whatever God's will for each of us might be, even if it's a life of service, it won't be boring or unfulfilling. We were created with an intense, built-in desire to live life to its fullest—to operate at peak performance. God makes himself available to help us achieve the potential he created within us. It's because we sense that potential that we expect so much of life. Intuitively we want to be all that God created us to be.

> Then God said, "Let us make man in our image, in our like-ness, and let them rule over the fish of the sea and the birds of the air, over the livestock, over all the earth, and over all the creatures that move along the ground." So God created man in his own image, in the image of God he created him; male and female he created them. (Genesis 1:26–27)

What *is* the image of God? Mediocre? Bored? Despondent? Hedonistic? On the contrary, he is the epitome of creativity, pro-ductivity, and adventure. Take a careful look at his creative work. Despite their efforts to deny his existence, every day scientists and scholars discover incredible purpose and design in nature. Our meager understanding has only scratched the surface of the awesome magnitude of creation.

In the realm of emotion and relationships, he is no less than magnificent. His love knows no bounds. Forty-one times, Scripture says, "His love endures forever." In our behalf, he can perform miracles that go beyond the physical laws he set in place. In the words of a popular song, "Our God is an awesome God."

It would be easy to be so overwhelmed by his greatness that we consider ourselves totally insignificant—a belief that per-meates some circles of Christianity—except for one often for-gotten, life-changing truth: *he* did not consider us insignificant. This all-powerful, magnificent God created you and me *in his own image*![1]

In what way are we made in God's image? For one thing, God chose to share with us some of his own awesome knowl-edge and ability. He allows us, for instance, a limited under-standing of the world he has created. In addition, he makes himself available in a saving relationship with you and me, a relationship that makes possible an ever-increasing revelation of himself and his creation. He even gives us the opportunity to demonstrate to others, through our lives, his love. That alone makes life worth living and should provide us with great fulfillment and gusto.

Everything in Scripture indicates that God wants us to get, even in this earthly life, all the gusto for which we were created. Jesus said, "I have come that they may have life, and have it to the full" (John 10:10).

No wonder we yearn for something more than the mundane rut we often settle into. Like the general who has fought in great battles but now sits behind a desk, we ache to be where the action is. We long for meaning and significance in our lives. And we yearn to regain some of the godlike image of our original creation. We can't help it. God's creative potential courses through our veins. The knowledge and the hope of "what is not but could be" is programmed into our souls. We know there is more.

No, the desire for a fulfilling life isn't evil. It is, in fact, born of our spiritual heritage—one of the signs that we were created by God. We have the engine of a race car and live the life of a station wagon (wood-paneled sides and all). No wonder we're vulnerable to ads that promise gusto living! We were *designed* for gusto living!

So Where's the Gusto?

If we were programmed by God to yearn for excellence, for the abundant life—then *where is it*? Was it all just a cosmic joke on God's part? Why did God design us to crave excellence, and then surround us with mediocrity? Obviously, something has gone very wrong. But who blew it?

The truth is that we have tried to satisfy the deepest yearnings of our hearts with counterfeits. Way back at the beginning, with Adam, we decided that we could do better without the

Creator. We eliminated from our lives the best things, thinking we could find something even better. Now we're engaged in a desperate search for that "something better," looking in all the wrong places. We've chosen the wrong definition of *gusto*. We spend entire lifetimes lunging for the golden ring, which we think will bring fulfillment and purpose, only to find—when we finally get our little fingers around it—that the gold ring is a cheap imitation of the real thing, and we're left emptier and more unfulfilled than before.

What are these imitations we've settled for?

One is our pursuit of leisure. Many people spend years trying to reach a place in life where they can coast, where no pain or trouble can find them. We call it retirement. Those who never reach that goal will die believing they missed out on the secret to happiness. Those who *do* reach it will often die of boredom and purposelessness. Statistics show that retirement can be deadly. Coasting kills. If the human species had been designed to coast, God would have made us with automatic transmissions and wheels. A good night's sleep and occasional relaxation is all the coasting we need.

The most satisfied, fulfilled people are those who can hardly wait to get up in the morning so they can put 'er in gear and get going. The most exciting retirees are those who define retirement as getting a new set of treads on the old tires so they can be ready for the next twenty-five thousand miles—"re-tired" and ready to go.

Financial security and affluence are two more counterfeits for gusto living. On the program *20/20,* Barbara Walters asked multimillionaire Ted Turner, "What is it like to be so wealthy and powerful?" I was amazed to hear this man—who has condemned Christianity as a religion for weak people—reply, "It's like an empty bag." Obviously, for at least one phenomenally wealthy man, affluence has not led to maximum living.

Gusto living is not a station in life—it's a state of mind. It doesn't come from living up to some society-designated measure of performance. It isn't defined by what others expect of you, and you don't find it by comparing your own accomplishments to what others have done. Instead, it's found in living with the knowledge that you are operating at your own peak performance, using the gifts and abilities God gave you to their full intended extent. Does living in this way bring you comfort, fame, or giddy happiness? Not necessarily. But it just might bring you peace, purpose, and power.

Is This All There Is?

A song popular in the late sixties expresses the desperate question that burns in the hearts of so many men and women. After being disappointed by much of what the world promises, the singer asks:

> Is that all there is?
> Is that all there is, my friend?
> Then let's keep dancing.
> Let's break out the booze and have a ball.
> If that's all there is.

The answer to the sad question in that song is a resounding *no*! That is *not* all there is. There's more! Is life full of disappointments and struggles? Of course. Has sin robbed humankind of the full potential of original creation? Yes. But there is still hope. The battle is not over. God didn't design this earth to be just a waiting room for eternal life; eternal life begins at the moment Christ enters your life. There is so much to accomplish, so much to experience, so much fulfillment and potential available in *this* life.

How can you realize that potential? How can you fire up your life?

Let's find the answers to those questions together—in this book.

1. Acknowledging that we still bear the image of God does not refute the
   total depravity of man. As Ronald B. Allen is careful to point out, "If those
   who are fallen still bear God's image, then their [sinful] condition is wors-
   ened. When fallen people sin, and in their sin they still bear God's image,
   then their sin is all the more heinous" (Ronald B. Allen, *The Majesty of
   Man* [Portland, Ore.: Multnomah Press, 1984], 105).

Chapter 2
WHEEL OF MISFORTUNE

Sometimes our activity, our work, is
nothing more than a cheap imitation
to deaden the pain of an empty life.

—Adolf Coors IV

A Race Not Worth Running

Henry lay on his side, exhausted, a short distance from the mill. Only the rasping sound of his labored panting broke the still morning air.

Faintly Henry could recall the rush of adrenaline that had so long ago accompanied his first energetic steps toward the finish line he had assumed lay ahead of him. He couldn't remember when he had started running, though—and worse yet, he couldn't remember why he had been running. It had been so exciting in the beginning. But somewhere along the way, the exhilaration had been replaced with exhaustion and a numbing realization that crushed all hope: there was no finish line.

As he lay in the moist straw, Henry closed his eyes and allowed his breathing to slowly return to normal. In that rare moment of inactivity, he smelled the reality of the world around him for the first time in a long time. He took it all in—but only for a moment. A sound from the mill caught his attention, and he opened his eyes. He turned his head just in time to see the huge circular treadmill whine to a stop.

Slowly he sat up and stared at the machine that had dominated so much of his life. *This treadmill is killing you,* pleaded an ancient voice deep within him. *Don't waste another moment on this race.* As he drank deeply from the cool spring of water nearby, the voice triggered a dull ache in his heart. There had to be more to life than the machine offered. The cool water revived him, and his breathing slowed. He felt refreshed. Maybe he could start a new life. Maybe today! But how? What would he do next? Where would he go? What goals would he pursue?

Well, those decisions could come later. Right now he felt a little frightened by the prospect of change. Until he could work out the details, he would stick with the tried and true—and safe. So, still dreaming about things that could be, he unconsciously stepped onto the wheel for the thousandth time in his short life. Soon its mesmerizing whir and the reflected light flashing from the turning spokes blocked the pain. Freedom and adventure could wait. For now, the treadmill required no risk, no faith, no thought. He would live later. For now, he would just run.

If you haven't already figured it out, Henry is a hamster. Yet his life parallels that of many twentieth-century men and women. Caught on a treadmill of boredom and conformity, they see only glimpses of life's true possibilities. Those brief glimmers of hope are moments of opportunity—opportunity often lost because of the difficulty of breaking out of the vicious circle these men and women live in. Keeping the treadmill spinning keeps them too busy to plan purposeful change. Besides, charting a new course into an unknown future is scary—and the rat race, while monotonous, is at least safe.

In the beginning there was no rat race. But the starting gun for the rat race we run today was fired almost immediately—when Eve became dissatisfied with who she was. She wanted to be like somebody else. She wanted to be like God.

"'You will not surely die,' the serpent said to the woman. 'For God knows that when you eat of it your eyes will be opened, and *you will be like God,* knowing good and evil.' When the woman saw that the fruit of the tree was good for food and pleasing to the eye, and also desirable for gaining wisdom, she took some and ate it. She also gave some to her husband, who was with her, and he ate it" (Genesis 3:4–6, emphasis added).

As she swallowed the first bite of forbidden fruit, the tread-mill creaked into motion. She and her mate laid the foundation for the mediocre lives so many live today and created a pattern that most of us never find a way to break. Instead of becoming like God, as the serpent promised, Adam and Eve took a huge step backward. Doubt took over where confidence had once ruled. Suspicion and envy set up camp in their minds and polluted the spotless ecology of their hearts. The wheel picked up speed, spinning faster and faster as Adam and Eve and all their descendants lost sight of their true worth and began looking for evidence of their value in all the wrong places.

Who Invented the Wheel?

Whenever we lose sight of God, we lose sight of our God-given worth and value. Without a sense of worth, we lose our sense of dignity and purpose. And without dignity and purpose, we lose our will to live. In their book *Why America Doesn't Work,* Chuck Colson and Jack Eckerd explain this principle:

> During World War II, those Jews who were not immediately exterminated by Hitler's brutal henchmen were herded into disease-infested concentration camps. In Hungary the Nazis set up a camp factory where prisoners were forced to distill tons of human waste and garbage into alcohol to be used as fuel additive. Perhaps even worse than being forced to labor amid the nauseating odor of stewing sludge was the prisoners' realization that their work was helping to fuel the

Führer's war machine. Yet month after month the laborers survived on meager food and disgusting work.

In 1944 Allied aircraft began bold air strikes deep into Europe. One night this area of Hungary was bombed, and the hated factory destroyed. The next morning the guards ordered the prisoners to one end of the charred remains where they were commanded to shovel the debris into carts and drag it to the other end of the compound.

They're going to make us rebuild this place, the prisoners thought as they bent to their labor.

The next day they were ordered to move the huge pile of debris again, back to the other end of the compound.

Stupid swine, the prisoners murmured to themselves. *They made a mistake and now we have to undo everything we did yesterday.*

But it was no mistake.

Day after day the prisoners hauled the same mountain of rubble back and forth from one end of the camp to the other.

After several weeks of this meaningless drudgery, one old man began sobbing uncontrollably and was led away by the guards. Another screamed until his captors beat him into silence. Then a young man who had survived three years of the vile labor that supported the oppressors' cause darted away from the group and raced toward the electrified fence.

"Halt!" the guards shouted. But it was too late. There was a blinding flash, a terrible sizzling noise, and the smell of smoldering flesh.

The futile labor continued, and in the days that followed dozens of prisoners went mad and ran from their work, only to be shot by the guards or electrocuted by the fence.

Their captors didn't care, of course. Indeed the commandant of the camp had ordered this monstrous activity as "an experiment in mental health" to see what would happen when people were given meaningless work. After seeing the results, he smugly remarked that at this rate there soon would be "no more need to use the crematoria."[1]

"If you want to utterly crush a man," said the great Russian novelist Fyodor Dostoyevsky in *The House of the Dead*, "just give him work of a completely senseless, irrational nature."

Dostoyevsky, who himself spent ten years in prison, wrote, "If he had to move a heap of earth from one place to another and back again—I believe the convict would hang himself ... preferring rather to die than endure ... such humiliation, shame, and torture.

"Deprived of meaningful work, men and women lose their reason for existence; they go stark, raving mad."

The people in Colson and Eckerd's example were prisoners of a brutal dictatorship. In today's world, people who are caught up in meaningless work are often prisoners of meaningless lives. When men and women are deprived of a meaningful life—when they go through the motions every day, over and over, without knowing the value or purpose of their daily activities—what do they do? Like those who had to move the dirt back and forth, they go mad.

What gives life meaning, then? The only rational explanation of what gives meaning and purpose to existence is this: We were created by an intelligent, purposeful, and loving God who designed the world with order and created us in his own image, making us capable of understanding the world we live in. Fortunately, that is the truth.

But throughout history, men and women have had trouble accepting this truth. Not because it is philosophically implausible; it is, in fact, the most plausible of all explanations. Rather, rebellious hearts reject this simple explanation because if, as the Bible claims, God does exist—and if he has redeemed us with Christ's blood—then he deserves our worship and allegiance. Unfortunately, humans have never been particularly anxious to worship anyone other than themselves. Therefore it is much more convenient (if less plausible) to explain human existence, and its purpose, without God. That way, we owe him nothing.

But the problem is this: When we make God meaningless, we remove the meaning from our own existence.

Who Stole the Finish Line?

While men and women have been running from God since Adam and Eve, modern man has gone a giant step further. Since the early twentieth century, the predominant philosophies—those that have permeated our educational and governmental systems—have openly proposed, or implied by omission, that our existence is a by-product of chance. Because we no longer believe that we were purposefully designed by a marvelous Creator, we have slowly come to believe that we have no purpose. Grade school children are taught that they are accidents of slimy algae. It's considered scientifically incorrect to talk about purpose and design. In many places, in fact, it is illegal to teach creationism. Proponents of the philosophies of purposelessness even examine each other's language to be sure that no implication of purposeful life slips through. In the "Letters" section of an issue of *Animal Kingdom* (a journal of biology), Dorothy H. Fader said she detected language of purpose or design (technically known as teleology) in John McLoughlin's article entitled "The Lost World." McLoughlin replied to Fader, "Teleology is the *erroneous* doctrine that living systems evolve toward an implied goal rather than changing in response to pressures around them. There is no evidence of the existence of goals in any evolutionary trend...."[2]

Look at what these men, who helped shape modern thought, have done to knock the foundations for meaningful living from our thinking:

> Man is the product of causes which had no prevision of the end they were achieving.... His origin, his growth, his hopes and fears, his loves and his beliefs, are but the outcome of accidental collocations of atoms ... and the whole temple

of man's achievement must inevitably be buried beneath the debris of a universe in ruins. . . .

Brief and powerless is man's life; on him and all his race the slow, sure doom falls pitiless and dark. Blind to good and evil, reckless of destruction, omnipotent matter rolls on its relentless way.[3]

Since we are merely a collection of molecules ourselves, there is no "we" apart from molecules. Our behavior consists of some molecules moving other molecules around.[4]

The title of a book by Richard Dawkins, one of the most respected astronomers of our day, says it all: *The Blind Watchmaker: Why Evidence Reveals a Universe Without Design.*[5]

B. F. Skinner, a man who had a profound influence on philosophy and psychology, said:

We are told that what is threatened is "man qua man," or "man in his humanity," or "man as Thou not It," or "man as a person not a thing." . . . What is being abolished is autonomous man . . . the man defended by the literatures of freedom and dignity.

His abolition has long been overdue. . . . To man qua man we readily say good riddance.[6]

According to this worldview (which is still the basis of our educational philosophy), we are simply accidents of nature, coming from nowhere and going nowhere. Clearly, the scene is set for extreme dissatisfaction and lack of fulfillment. For a hundred years, we have been laying the philosophical foundation for misery. Even the purveyors of these ideas recognized that only hopelessness and death would result from them. Bertrand Russell summed up his own godless philosophy well when he said, "There is darkness without and when I die there will be darkness within. There is no splendor, nor vastness anywhere; only triviality for a moment and then nothing."

When you take away humanity's only reasonable explanation

for a meaningful and purposeful life, humanity writhes in pain, casting about for the smallest hope, searching for evidence of personal worth and value—and chasing after every elusive and empty promise that we think might give us that worth.

The attempt to explain the world without God is the course upon which the rat race is run—and, sadly, there is no finish line.

Who Needs Self-Esteem?

The subtitle of this book is *Living with Nothing to Prove, Nothing to Hide, and Nothing to Lose*. Why do so many of us live our lives feeling that we have something to prove? Because we have no sense of personal value—and therefore no self-esteem. We feel we have to prove—through accomplishments, through wealth, through power—that we are worth something.

This concept immediately raises flags in the minds of some Christians who think of self-esteem as sinful. But self-esteem is not a sin; to the contrary, we lose our self-esteem *because* of sin. Self-esteem is a by-product of knowing where we came from, why we are here, and where we are going. I've heard Christian leaders suggest that self-esteem is a humanistic idea not worthy of consideration by Christians. They say, "Without God we are nothing." They are correct. But Christians are *not* "without God." We belong to him, and we were created by him in his own image—and that fact alone gives us value and should enable us to have a positive self-image.

> Self-worth pertains to a man's belief and conviction that he has a fundamental value . . . because he is created in God's image. Pride pertains to the pleasure a man finds in himself for what he believes he can or what he has achieved or accomplished with his life. . . . A fundamental sense of self-worth draws a person closer to God; the sin of pride leads a man to self-worship: he seeks to usurp the rightful throne of God.[7]

Webster's Dictionary defines the word *esteem* this way: "to prize; to set a high value on; to have a high regard for or a favorable opinion of." That is a perfect description of how God feels about us. If *we* are created in *his* image and are still without value, as some would suggest, then we cast grave suspicion on *his* value. And that, of course, is ridiculous.

Imagine that God were to introduce man to a group of religious teachers:

> "This is my creation," God explains, guiding man forward for their inspection. "He is fearfully and wonderfully made in my own image. He has sinned and no longer demonstrates the glory of my original creation, but I love him dearly and have sacrificed my Son to redeem his soul."
>
> "You think he is valuable?" the religious leaders exclaim. "*This* creature? Yuck! It would be *sinful* to consider man as valuable!"
>
> What a slap in the face of God to believe that man, created in God's image and redeemed through the sacrifice of God's son, Jesus, is worthless.
>
> "But didn't man's fall so tarnish the image of God in us that it's basically unrecognizable?" you might be asking. It's true that our sin has taken much of the power and joy from God's original creation, but neither Adam's sin, devastating as it was, nor our own continuing sin, succeeded in wiping out God's image in us.
>
> "We are in danger of overstating the results of the Fall if we judge that man after the Fall is no longer a creature of dignity bearing the image of God."[8]

We also have Scripture's promise that God will continue to work to restore us to the glory of our original creation and beyond: "Dear friends, now we are children of God, and what we will be has not yet been made known. But we know that when he appears, we shall be like him, for we shall see him as he is. Everyone who has this hope in him purifies himself, just as he is pure" (1 John 3:2–3).

We were created like God, and he intends that we will some-day be like him again. We may not now be everything that he originally created us to be, but we are still his creation. After he had finished forming Adam and Eve, he looked at his handiwork and proclaimed, "It is good." Then we humans brought the blight of sin into his beautiful creation, but still he did not aban-don us as worthless. His authorship of our being was not inval-idated. Instead he offered his Son to redeem us, thereby demonstrating his love for us. It is true that we cannot be good or have value in and of ourselves. But the question is moot, because we cannot be considered in and of ourselves. Nothing can change the fact that we are his creation. Nothing can destroy the evidence that he chose to save us. Nothing can take away the value that he himself assigned to us.

> In spite of the loss of communion with God and the impair-ment of their natures, fallen people remain in God's likeness as living and active personal spirits. Human beings continue to be of great value.... No human should be murdered, because every man and woman remains in God's image metaphysically (Genesis 9:6). And because everyone remains in the image of God, we ought not even curse people. (James 3:9)[9]

Christianity has been criticized as having a low view of humanity. To the contrary, it is the secular worldview that diminishes the value of people. Believers in Christ should never be found denying the truth that God's sacrifice established. Before the Fall, Adam and Eve knew exactly who they were— they were creations of a magnificent God. They didn't have to consult psychiatrists to "find themselves." And because they daily walked so closely with God, they were in no danger of for-getting that wonderful truth. The entire universe was at their feet. They were so surrounded by the knowledge of his love that they had no reason to question their worth.

Only when they turned away from God in disobedience did their self-image take a nosedive. They instantly devalued themselves in their own eyes. They even became ashamed of their own bodies. But *God did not devalue them.* Nor did he stop loving them. He was prepared even at the moment of their rebellion to offer the supreme sacrifice to redeem their souls. In that sacrifice, he would reconfirm the value he had given them in the first place. After all, God did not love Adam and Eve because they were worth loving. Rather, because he loved them, they had worth.

Nevertheless, their act of turning from God began a pattern that has repeated itself through history. And we no longer just ignore God; now we have philosophies that lead entire generations in a defiant path directly opposed to the truth that could set them free. Not only have humans turned from God, they have also made a concerted effort to distance themselves from him— and the further you get from God, the more you lose sight of your true value. Our stubborn resistance to God blinds us to the very truth that could save us. If we choose the dark route of trying to prove our worth, we'll waste a lifetime trying to prove what we should already know to be true. We *do* have value. And that value needs no proof, no evidence beyond the cross.

We have nothing to prove.

A Runner I Once Knew

Looking back at our lives, nearly all of us can identify incidents that crystallized our feelings of insecurity, that damaged our self-esteem immensely. It may have been a careless comment from an insensitive person. It may have been an effort that failed miserably—especially damaging if it happened in front of others—or a social gaffe that resulted in great embarrassment. It may have been childhood injustice or abuse.

We can empower these memories to keep us on the treadmill for life. There are two ways to empower them. First, we empower them by ignoring the effect they have had on our lives—and by refusing to acknowledge this effect and refusing to seek healing from it. Second, and worse, we can give these memories absolute power by believing that we are the powerless victims of these events and that they alone are responsible for our behaviors and attitudes.

I have total recall of one of those moments. It was the day that hand-eye coordination tests were held in my physical education class at high school. Each student would be required to catch a football three times, each time while running in a different direction. The final grade for the semester would rest on how well we performed.

I knew I was in trouble. I had the hand-eye coordination of a carp. And because of a physical deformity—curvature of the bone in both arms, which restricted my movement—I couldn't catch a football while standing still, let alone while running.

I can still feel the humid breath of stale air that hung over the athletic field that day. I can see how it stirred the sandy hair of the boy in front of me in line. His name was Daniel, and he was built like Hercules. Daniel had muscles in places I didn't even have places. As he stepped forward to take his turn, I swallowed hard, knowing I would be next. Daniel ran to the left and caught with ease the ball thrown by the young substitute instructor. He also caught the next pass while running to the right. Then he ran down the field for the long pass. Running at full speed, Daniel watched over his shoulder as the ball spiraled toward him, then reached up at the last possible moment and snatched it from the air. The momentum of the ball caused him to stumble, but he quickly regained his balance and, with one hand, waved the ball above his head in victory.

I couldn't even *hold* the ball in one hand, let alone wave it. I heard my name and stepped forward. I knew I wouldn't be able to catch the ball. At that moment, I wished that my curvature of the bone were more noticeable; maybe the young P.E. instructor would have been more sympathetic. As it was, his intensity made it seem as if passing this test was a life-and-death matter.

The first time it was thrown, the ball actually hit my hands as I stumbled to the left. I thought that was pretty miraculous in itself. Unfortunately, I couldn't turn my palms flat enough to pull it in.

As I ran to the right I almost caught it. In slow motion the ball danced at the end of my outstretched hands, tempting me with success—then it fell to the ground about the same time I did.

I never even saw the long pass until it was bouncing in front of me.

"Hit the showers," the instructor growled without looking at me. "You'll never amount to anything."

You'll never amount to anything.

If he had known the effect those words would have on me, I don't think he would have ever uttered them.

I tried to block out the laughter as I walked what seemed like a hundred miles to the locker-room door. Standing in the shower, I was grateful for the cascading water that camouflaged my tears. Probably what the instructor had meant was that I would never be a good football player, but in my mind, his words applied to my entire life. I didn't think of his words as cruel. I thought of them as true. How could anyone with such authority and athletic ability be wrong? I wept not because I couldn't catch a football but because I thought I lacked some valuable life ingredient that God had graciously bestowed on most other people but had forgotten or neglected to give to me. I was measuring my worth by a false standard, and I didn't measure up. I couldn't run fast, I was uncomfortable with the opposite sex, I wasn't athletic, and I wasn't exceptionally bright. I really believed what my coach told me: I would never amount to anything.

And that day, I began a desperate quest to prove to the world (myself included) that I was worth something, that my life had some redeeming value. It's a quest that you may be on as well; it's a quest undertaken by anyone who lives to prove his or her worth. And it's a quest that begins on a foundation of quicksand.

That was not, of course, the only incident in my young life that put my self-worth in question. It was only one of a group of incidents that became painfully significant due to one simple reason: I lacked a solid foundation from which to judge my own worth. The quest for self-worth, in itself, presupposes a perceived lack of worth. Deep down, I already saw myself as worthless.

Unfortunately, it would be many years before I finally gained an understanding of what gave my life value. The search would cost me a great deal of wasted time, personal agony, and missed opportunities. For a time, it warped my view of God and of his love. Nevertheless, I am grateful—it could have destroyed my life, as it has destroyed the lives of others.

No Discounts on God's People

Why do people set out to prove their worth? Because they are trying desperately to discredit their *own* secret belief that they are indeed worthless. Deep down, even before my coach's comment, I believed that I was worthless. Yet I determined in my heart to find a way to prove us both wrong—not just to *prove* my worth but to *gain* worth.

People who are aware of their own worth, and of why they have that value, have nothing to prove to anybody. Instead they demonstrate with their lives every day, without particularly trying to, what they already know to be true—that God loves them and has an important role for them to play in life.

People who lack that understanding of our unique and intrinsic worth are vulnerable to every perceived failure, every careless comment. They are condemned to a reactive existence that is light years from their true potential.

Unfortunately, the temptation to waste your life in these pursuits doesn't go away with age. As James Dobson states in his best-seller *Hide or Seek:*

> Teenagers are by no means alone in this personal deval-
> uation. Every age poses its own unique threats to self-

esteem.... Little children typically suffer severe loss of status during the tender years of childhood. Likewise, most adults are still attempting to cope with the inferiority experienced in earlier times.[10]

Wisdom, experience, and a growing understanding of God's love can decrease the seductive call to live with something to prove, but they never banish it completely. Even today I am constantly reminded of how feelings of inferiority affect my own actions. Even the memories of my school years are skewed by false perceptions of worth. My teachers weren't cruel people intent upon destroying my psyche forever, but that's the way I remember many of them. My feelings of inadequacy led me to interpret even their smallest rebuffs as more evidence of my sorry existence.

For years, I told people that the words written beneath my picture in the senior yearbook were "Class Clown"—words that I interpreted as just another jab at my character. Recently I found that yearbook. Written beneath my picture are the complimentary words "Most Talented." Poor self-esteem is a powerful psychological force; it can twist our memories into falsehoods that suit its purposes.

In those early years, I put every ounce of my effort into trying to find someone or something that would bestow value on my life. It was a fruitless effort. Yes, I accomplished a few things, but those golden nuggets of recognition slipped through my fingers like sand. There is no one on the face of the earth capable of bestowing worth on you or me, no accomplishment that will bring, once and for all, the sense of value that we instinctively know must be there.

After the Fall

Ten years after I graduated from high school, I returned to my school to serve as the commencement speaker for a new graduating class. I was no longer the frightened, insecure person

I had been when I graduated. I had lifted weights for six years and gained about thirty solid pounds. To prepare for the reunion, I had lain on a beach for weeks to get a tan (not an easy task in northern Minnesota). I wanted all those girls who had rejected me to regret what they had missed.

And it wasn't just my physical appearance that had been rejuvenated; my whole life had changed. I had begun the journey of abundant living. The renewed confidence and purpose in my life were unmistakable.

The speaker's platform was six feet high, built of plywood and two-by-fours. Behind the platform, strips of crepe paper hung from the ceiling, serving as a backdrop. As I stepped onto that platform, the faces of many of my old classmates and teachers seasoned the audience. That day will live in my mind forever. I delivered one of the most emotionally powerful speeches of my life. When I concluded, the audience rose in a standing ovation. With the sweet sound of applause ringing in my ears, I moved to the back of the stage and sat on the folding chair reserved for me.

I was in a trance of joy. Then, beneath the sounds of applause, a small, evil voice whispered a lie—a lie that same voice has whispered in slightly different versions to millions throughout the ages. "This is it," he crooned, gesturing toward the audience. "This is what makes your life worth living. This is what gives you worth." I might have fallen for that deceptive line had it not been for a marvelous God with a wonderful sense of humor. Evidently, he saw my peril, reached down, and gently touched my chair. The back legs of that folding chair slipped off the back of the stage, and I went through the curtain of crepe paper and fell six feet to the ground.

The applause stopped. Some in the audience had actually seen me fall. They were convinced I must be dead. Others had turned to a friend, or blinked, and missed the fall. They had no idea where I had gone—I had simply disappeared.

As I lay behind the stage in that overwhelming silence, the voice came again. This time the owner of that voice pointed his bony finger in my face and hissed, "Your P.E. teacher was right. You'll never amount to anything. You blow every opportunity that comes your way. You are worth exactly nothing."

That moment hangs frozen in time. It was one of those moments upon which destiny swings. I could succumb to the lying accusations of the Destroyer and let that memory become one more piece of evidence that he was right, or I could move forward in the power of the truth. I made the right choice. I broke his bony finger and began to laugh, and I haven't stopped since.

What truth saved me in that embarrassing moment? The same truth that will keep you from living with something to prove: the truth that our worth has nothing to do with our performance. God didn't love me any less as I was lying in a heap behind the stage than he did when I'd been standing on the platform basking in the standing ovation. Nor was my worth tied to my improved physical appearance or to the fact that, at this point in my life, I was doing well enough to be invited to be a commencement speaker. My worth was tied directly to God's love. And God's love is indestructible. That was the truth that freed me to laugh out loud. I thought, *Why should I be embarrassed? I know where I am. It's the people in the audience who are confused!*

I peeked up from behind the stage. Everyone was frozen in midapplause, their hands held up as if indicating the size of their latest fish. There is no ceremonious way to climb back up on a six-foot stage. I threw one leg up, heaved the rest of my body onto the stage, then rolled over and stood up. They gave me another ovation! Then I moved to the microphone and told them what I had neglected to tell them the first time—that it wasn't lifting weights or lying on a beach or traveling around the country to speak that had so dramatically changed me. It was the unconditional love of God, demonstrated by Jesus Christ. He had bestowed worth on my unworthy soul. He had replaced fear with confidence, replaced sadness and shame with laughter.

For the same reason that I now recognize that I have personal value, I know that you also have great personal value—and not because of anything you've accomplished, not because of how much money you earn, not because of how famous or attractive you are. You have value because of Jesus Christ. You have value because he made you. You have value because he made you unique. You have value because he loved you in spite of your sin. You have value because he paid the supreme price for your redemption. You have value because no matter how you may have ignored him, no matter how heinous the sins you have committed, no matter how people measure your contribution to society, he loves you—because you are his.

You have nothing to prove. Your worth was initiated at Creation and guaranteed on the cross.

Don't live to prove you have worth. *Because* you have worth—*live!*

1. Charles Colson and Jack Eckerd, *Why America Doesn't Work* (Dallas: Word, 1991), xi–xii.
2. Fader's question and McLoughlin's response is in the "Letters" section of *Animal Kingdom* (July–August 1987), 7, 54. The original article in question is John C. McLoughlin, "The Lost World," *Animal Kingdom* (January–February 1987), 6–7, 46–47. Emphasis added.
3. Bertrand Russell as quoted by Colin Chapman, *The Case for Christianity* (Grand Rapids: Eerdmans, 1981), 226.
4. Philip B. Applewhite, *Molecular Gods: How Molecules Determine Our Behavior* (Englewood Cliff, N.J.: Prentice-Hall, 1981), 2.
5. Richard Dawkins, *The Blind Watchmaker: Why Evidence Reveals a Universe Without Design* (New York: W. W. Norton, 1986).
6. B. F. Skinner, *Beyond Freedom and Dignity* (New York: Alfred A. Knopf, 1971), 200.
7. Wayland O. Ward, "Self-Image, Pride, and Self-Love," *Counseling Communique* (January–February, 1980), 1.
8. Ronald B. Allen, *The Majesty of Man* (Portland, Ore.: Multnomah Press, 1984), 104.
9. Gordon R. Lewis and Bruce A. Demarest, *Integrative Theology*, vol. 2 (Grand Rapids: Zondervan, 1990), 209.
10. James Dobson, *Hide or Seek* (Old Tappan, N.J.: Revell, 1974), 11.

Chapter 3
A REASON FOR LIVING

There once was a teacher
Whose principal feature
Was hidden in quite an odd way.
Students by the millions
Or possibly zillions
Surrounded him all of the day.
When finally seen
By his scholarly dean
And asked how he managed the deed,
He lifted three fingers
And said, "All you swingers
Need only to follow my lead.
To rise from a zero
To big Campus Hero,
To answer these questions you'll strive:
Where am I going,
How shall I get there, and
How will I know I've arrived?"[1]

My dad, a World War II veteran, is a survivor of the Baton death march and an ex-POW. In August 1945, after three and a half years of brutal confinement in a Japanese prison camp, he and his weakened, starving fellow prisoners were liberated. Planes flew over and dropped barrels of food. One of the barrels fell near my father and burst open, propelling hundreds of candy bars in every direction and sending prisoners scrambling to gather them up. But rather than eating their fill, many ran about stuffing the candy bars into their clothes, automatically following the habit of a prisoner: hoarding for the time when there would be hunger again. These men were free; they undoubtedly would soon return stateside. The prison guards had disappeared at the first word of Japanese surrender. A banquet of delights that these prisoners had only been able to dream about for the past three and a half years would soon be theirs again. But they had been prisoners for so long that they were unprepared to take advantage of their newfound freedom. They behaved as though they were still held captive.

A motivational speaker told me of a similar experience. He too had been held prisoner. His cell was a cramped, fetid stone dungeon only four paces wide. Day after day he would pace the four steps to the wet stone wall and back. When he finally stepped from the darkness of his prison into the bright sunlight after years of captivity, he took four steps—and stopped, afraid to go on. He had grown accustomed to a world four paces wide. Now he would have to deal with the unknown challenges that came from being able to take as many paces as he wished. He looked over his shoulder, and for just a moment, the four-pace cell beckoned, safe and familiar. Then he shook off the fear and began to run. He could manage only a clumsy, ungainly, stumbling gait, but in his mind he ran like a wild horse on the open prairie.

The point of these stories, of course, is that after you have lived within the suffocating limitations of the treadmill, it can be a terrifying experience to shake off those limitations and regain your freedom. Freedom is indeed frightening. Like the soldier who, after years of military service, accepted his discharge and returned to civilian life only to reenlist after a few months because he didn't know how to live without someone telling him what to do, we face the danger of deciding to return to the treadmill out of fear and lack of direction. After all, the routine of a mundane existence is at least safe and predictable. You may not find yourself on the same treadmill you were on before, but the world is full of treadmills. And if you don't know where you are going, the world will drag you where it is going.

A cartoon in our newspaper showed a cat releasing all the animals from a pet shop. "Be free!" he proclaimed as he opened cage after cage. But the frightened animals, perhaps wondering who would feed them outside or what dangers lay out there, would not leave. Slamming the doors to their cages, the cat walked away disgusted. "Then be secure!" he muttered.

Those of us who have decided to lay aside a destructive pattern of living and be free—to step outside that cage door—find ourselves facing a definite lack of security. "What do I do now?" we ask. "What goals do I set? How can I begin to implement this new freedom in my life?" There are three questions that a person must answer to ensure that he or she will never again run on a treadmill created by someone else:

What is my purpose in life?
What are the principles that will guide my quest to fulfill that purpose?
What plan or goals will get me there?

Whatever Thou Doest, Doest It on Purpose

Nietzsche said, "If we possess our why of life we can put up with almost any how."[2]

Most people do not *live* life. They simply let life *happen* to them. Like passive victims, they become prisoners of their past, slaves to the circumstances of the present, and fearful of the future. People who live with gusto are men and women who live with purpose. For them life is more than just reacting to whatever comes. Life is the vehicle to accomplish something significant. People who live with purpose make a lasting impact on their world. The truth of that principle is so powerful that even people with evil purposes make it work for them, leaving a lasting *evil* impact on the world.

Most of us, although we sometimes take baby steps in the right direction, rarely run life's race with true freedom. Too often we start running before we know why or where. Consider, for instance, the emphasis we put on goals. Goal setting has become big business in America. On any given day, there are hundreds of seminars in session, teaching American executives and professionals how to set and achieve goals. Those who attend these seminars are usually motivated people seeking to make their lives purposeful and productive. But for those who want to live to full potential, goal setting is the wrong place to start.

Don't misunderstand me. I believe that goal setting is essential to productive life. But I also believe that goals are a means to an end, not an end in themselves. Until you have a clear idea of what *end* you want to accomplish, your goals will lack direction.

> To begin with an end [a purpose for living] in mind means to start with a clear understanding of your destination. It means to know where you're going so that you better understand where you are now and so that the steps you take [the goals you set] are always in the right direction....
> When you begin with the end in mind, you gain a different perspective.[3]

Those who plan their lives by setting goals without an ultimate purpose in mind are like a dog chasing his tail. They just go in circles. Even if the dog manages to catch his tail and chomp down, he'll be disappointed with his achievement (not to mention a trifle sore). Fido will still be left with the question, What do I do now?

A lost man counting his steps through the forest gets nowhere. A goal-oriented life without purpose is a life destined for disappointment. Most goals (I want to own a house, I want to be promoted to manager, I want to be a community leader) are too small and confining to be worthy of an entire life. They can easily be thwarted by circumstance. And even when they are achieved, it quickly becomes evident that they produce nothing like the joy and satisfaction we expected. Like the dog who has finally caught his tail, we're left disappointed and wondering, What now?

If you want to get the most out of life, it is essential that you first discover a purpose worth living for. With that purpose in mind, you can set goals that will consistently lead toward that end. A purpose-oriented life will be a life full of exciting goals.

Webster's Dictionary defines purpose as "that which a person sets before himself as an object to be reached or accomplished; aim; intention; design." John W. Alexander, in his book *Managing Our Work,* puts it this way:

> A purpose is a broad statement of an aspiration. It describes the general direction in which we desire to go. *A goal,* on the other hand, is a still more specific statement of what is to be accomplished to produce progress toward an objective.[4] The difference, then, between purpose and goal: A goal is measurable. It answers when it will be accomplished and how one knows that it has happened.[5]

Picture the opportunities of your life as a ladder. The purpose you choose for living is the star against which your ladder will rest, as in figure 1. Living without purpose is like carrying a ladder with no place to lean it.

Figure 1

When my father was first captured, he was amazed at the determination and "will to live" demonstrated by many of his fellow prisoners. Those men survived under conditions that would have killed most people. Malaria and dysentery ravaged their starving bodies, yet they made it. They had a purpose, a reason, to go on living—and live they did, surviving against unbelievable odds.

Equally amazing, though, was how quickly death came to the men who lost their will to live and their purpose for living. Some of them died within weeks of capture, even though there was nothing physically wrong with them. Some died in their sleep; some just withered away. Did they die for no reason? No! I think they died *because they had no reason*—no reason to live.

They undoubtedly had goals when they went into battle—to take the hill, perhaps, or maybe just to live through it. But those goals, without some larger purpose to strengthen them, had been defeated by the horror of prison camp, and those purposeless men had nothing bigger to hang on to. They allowed their present circumstances to strip them of all hope. Later, looking back, my dad said that he recalled no prisoner who had lost his will to live who made it back alive. Yet many others—starved, beaten, and diseased—nevertheless lived to go home, because their purpose for living gave them strength and hope.

Viktor Frankl's prison-camp experience paralleled my father's. When counseling his fellow prisoners, Frankl found that he could encourage a healthy, life-giving attitude in them "by pointing out a future goal to which they could look forward.... It is a peculiarity of man that he can only live by looking to the future.... The prisoner who had lost faith in the future—his future—was doomed. With his loss of belief in the future, he also lost his spiritual hold; he let himself decline and became subject to mental and physical decay."[6]

Without purpose, people die. Even if they don't physically die, they stop living. In today's society, many are dead and don't know it, since they've never tasted real life. During the Vietnam protests, a young man was seen holding up a sign that read "Nothing is worth dying for." The truth is that until you find something worth dying for, nothing will be worth living for. Purpose gives to your goals direction, motivation, and meaning. Purpose is the target at which goals are aimed. The more worthy your purpose for living, the more directed and powerful your goals will be. *Where there is purpose, there is power.*

The apostle Paul had a profound role in the spread of Christianity. Wherever he went, he impacted lives. His writings continue to influence millions of people today. His purpose was perfectly clear and unshakable. He said, *"I press on toward the goal to win the prize for which God has called me heavenward in Christ Jesus"* (Philippians 3:14, emphasis added).

Now *that* is an expression of the highest purpose in life. There is no greater achievement than to live to the fullest potential for which we were created—to be everything God created us to be. Although that general goal is the same for all humankind, each individual is designed to live it out in a unique way.

Many of the problems we face with self-esteem, much of the emptiness found in our busy lives—these things can be traced directly to the lack of this kind of purpose in our lives. Wealth, fame, love, and even the pursuit of happiness pale in the face of such focused living. Nothing can deter the man or woman who lives for a worthy purpose. He or she might be temporarily distracted, but once a person has experienced the crystal clarity of purposeful living, the fuzziness of distracted meandering and meaningless activity are unacceptable.

Ya Gotta Have Faith

I once asked a businessman if he knew what God's will was for his life. He shook his head in scorn. "I wouldn't stake my life on something as nebulous as 'God's will,'" he said. "I have a specific, concrete purpose for my life. I work for a powerful, important company, and it's my purpose to work my way right to the

top." His company made high-tech equipment for space explo-
ration. Three weeks after our discussion, that company initiated
massive cutbacks, and the businessman's job disappeared in a
cloud of managerial dust. Suddenly his whole reason for living
was gone. His purpose had been too small.

In contrast, look at the men and women of faith honored in
the eleventh chapter of the book of Hebrews—people who had
a larger purpose than that businessman, a purpose like Paul's.
They had their eyes fixed on God's will for their lives and on the
promises he had set before them. That kind of focus enabled
them to press on in the face of unbelievable odds. Many of those
people never personally saw the promises fulfilled. But their purpose for living was so powerful that it didn't matter. Their purpose was worthy of every struggle they endured, including death.
Obviously, they didn't consider God's will to be "nebulous."

The Bible calls this lifestyle "living by faith." And faith is
defined in the first verse of Hebrews 11: "Now faith is being sure
of what we hope for and certain of what we do not see."

Some of the people listed in that eleventh chapter of
Hebrews, the "Faith Hall of Fame," lived to see the triumphant
results of their faith:

> I do not have time to tell about Gideon, Barak, Samson, Jeph-
> thah, David, Samuel and the prophets, who through faith
> conquered kingdoms, administered justice, and gained what
> was promised; who shut the mouths of lions, quenched the
> fury of the flames, and escaped the edge of the sword; whose
> weakness was turned to strength; and who became powerful
> in battle and routed foreign armies. Women received back
> their dead, raised to life again. (Hebrews 11:32–35)

But not all of them saw such victory. God does not promise
that a focused life of faith will be easy, nor that it will be successful by worldly standards.

> Others were tortured and refused to be released, so that they
> might gain a better resurrection. Some faced jeers and flog-

ging, while still others were chained and put in prison. They were stoned; they were sawed in two; they were put to death by the sword. They went about in sheepskins and goatskins, destitute, persecuted and mistreated. (Hebrews 11:35–37)

Is it worth it to expend the effort and self-discipline to live with such focused purpose if our only reward is this kind of punishment? Evidently the men and women who lived it in Hebrews 11 felt it was, and most certainly God did. Listen again:

The world was not worthy of them. They wandered in deserts and mountains, and in caves and holes in the ground. These were all commended for their faith, yet none of them received what had been promised. *God had planned something better for us so that only together with us would they be made perfect.* (Hebrews 11:38–40, emphasis added)

How great was the power of this kind of purposeful life? Here's the answer: "All these people were still living by faith when they died" (Hebrews 11:13).

How many people do you know who keep living focused, powerful lives right up to the end? Some fizzle out at the first disappointment. Others waste their potential by running in every direction, chasing dreams that aren't worthy of their effort. Look at what God said about those whose lives were dedicated to the original purpose he had in mind:

They did not receive the things promised; they only saw them and welcomed them from a distance. And they admitted that they were aliens and strangers on earth. People who say such things show that they are looking for a country of their own. If they had been thinking of the country they had left, they would have had opportunity to return. (Hebrews 11:13–15)

Return to what? To the *treadmill*? It's true that many of the Israelites who under Moses' leadership were freed from Egyptian slavery wanted to return to captivity when freedom brought difficulties. But not the men and women of Hebrews.

Instead, they were longing for a better country—a heavenly one. Therefore God is not ashamed to be called their God, for he has prepared a city for them. (Hebrews 11:16)

"That's just pie-in-the-sky thinking," a man said to me recently. I told him that there's nothing wrong with pie-in-the-sky thinking if there really is a pie in the sky. The most powerful purpose for living—seeking God's will and dedicating yourself to fulfilling it by faith—will take you beyond the realm of experience available to most people on this earth and put you within sight of what God will eventually make available to you, enabling you to taste a little heaven on earth.

God doesn't promise that life on earth will be a rose garden. Instead he promises us trials and tribulations—and he also promises us the power and endurance to run and finish an adventure-filled race entirely worthy of us. The people listed in the Hebrews "Hall of Faith" were not superheroes with supernatural power; they were ordinary, sinful men and women who chose to follow a God with unlimited power—the same God who can enable even imperfect people like you and me to live extraordinary lives.

What purpose in life will cause us to live that extraordinary life? What is it that's really worth dying for? Having a nice car or big house? Getting a big promotion? Achieving a particular social status? Or was Paul on the right track after all?

Look at the tremendous diversity allowed in Paul's expression of purpose. All of us look to the same God for the power and wisdom to live lives with meaning and purpose, yet God created each of us to live a unique life in order to fulfill that purpose. Your path will be different from mine and different from the person's down the street. Yet each of us has a purpose so worthy that a lifetime of energy expended in achieving it would not be wasted. Even though we will never see that purpose completely fulfilled on this earth, the beautiful truth is this: we *will* see it fulfilled. Remember that verse from 1 John in the previous chapter? Paul says, "Dear friends, now we are children of God, and what we will be has not yet been made known. But we know that when he appears, we shall be like him, for we shall see him as he is" (1 John 3:2).

What is your purpose for living? Is it worth dying for? Is it worth expending the few precious moments you have on this earth? Does it cause you to jump from bed each morning with excitement and challenge? Will it last? Maybe you live to build a business or a ministry. Maybe your purpose is to be a good parent or to make an impact of some kind in your community. Your purpose could be selfish or even evil—perhaps you live to satisfy an appetite for adventure, sexual gratification, or personal aggrandizement.

Any purpose will give your life more direction and power than no purpose at all. But the greatest and most productive purpose is to live to fulfill *God's* purpose for your life—to follow the manufacturer's recommendations for peak performance, to continue to press toward the mark of his high calling.

Ask yourself these questions:

What purpose do my actions indicate I am living for?
What purpose do my friends or my employer want me to live for?

Even though it may not be crystal clear exactly what actions God would have me take, am I committed to discovering his purpose for my life?

Am I willing to follow his leading as he reveals the details of his purpose to me?

If your answer to that last question is yes, now would be a perfect time to tell God you're ready, by praying something like:

I'm not perfect, Lord, but I want to press on to take hold of that for which Christ Jesus took hold of me. God, help me forget what is behind and strain toward what is ahead. Help me to press on toward the goal to win the prize for which God has called me heavenward in Christ Jesus. God, show me what you created me to do and be, and help me to begin to move toward that purpose in my life. Amen.

Now, if that is the purpose you desire for your life, think about the special gifts and abilities that God has given you. How, do you suppose, might God have enabled you, when he gave you those gifts and talents, to fulfill that purpose in a unique way?

Write down your unique purpose in life. You'll come back to this statement later, so make it as clear as you can.

My purpose in life is to:

_____

Keeping on Track

Remember Henry the hamster? As he lay gasping beside the treadmill, something deep within himself told him not to get back on it again. But he did. Life is a slippery road that slants toward destruction. It takes only a moment for the human heart to turn away from a loving God and a purposeful life and return to the treadmill of wasted effort.

Once we've stepped off the treadmill and discovered a purpose for living, what will keep us from going back to the treadmill? Principles. Life after the treadmill is guided not by routines, not by traditions, not by habits, but by principles. People who have discovered a reason for living feel a fire ignited in their souls; this fire drives them to action. Those actions must be guided by principles. I find it beautiful that the same God who by his love gives us a purpose for living also gives us the foundational principles that will allow us to move freely toward that purpose.

Remember the ladder you were carrying in figure 1? Principles are the sides of the ladder. They keep us focused on our purpose and headed in the right direction. They keep us from falling by the wayside by setting goals that will not contribute to our purpose for living. Figure 2 shows how it works.

There are two sets of principles that, when identified and followed, will provide our lives with a unifying direction that will keep them focused on our ultimate purpose. They are *univer-sal* principles and *unify-ing* principles.

Figure 2

Universal Principles

Universal principles were established by the Creator himself. They were designed for a per-fect world by a perfect God. Even though we live in a fallen world, those principles still apply. Our society, which resists moral absolutes, finds it difficult to accept the absolutes that God has set down in Scripture. As we'll discuss in chapter 7, it's important to remember that God didn't establish these guide-lines to restrict our joy in living or to keep us from experienc-ing life. Instead he gave us these guidelines to allow us to walk in close communion with him, constantly sensitive to the direc-tion of his will. These are the guidelines for maximum living—for *gusto* living.

The law was given to Israel after God had freed the Israelites after their four hundred years of slavery in Egypt. Referring to the Lord God of Israel as Yahweh, God's personal name, Vernard Eller imagines a conversation between God and the newly freed Israel:

Yahweh is saying in effect: "You are free men, right?"
"Right!"
"And it took me to get you that way, right?"
"Right!"
"I have rather adequately demonstrated that your free-
dom is my prime concern, right?"
"Right!"
"And having done what I did, I have proved myself to be
the world's leading expert on freedom, right?"
"Right!"
"Fine! Then let old Yahweh give you a few helpful tips on
how to be free men and stay that way, OK?"
The negativity of the commandments marks off small
areas into which free men ought not go—precisely so that
they can remain free to roam anywhere else in the great wide
world.[7]

Where are these universal principles recorded in Scripture?
The best-known ones are called the Ten Commandments. It may
have been a while since you last reviewed them—and no wonder; in our independence-crazy society, the Ten Commandments
are usually ridiculed as archaic and irrelevant. Yet imagine if we
could live in a world where everyone adhered to just these ten
(Exodus 20:3–17):

1. You shall have no other gods before me.
2. You shall not worship idols.
3. You shall not misuse the name of God.
4. Remember the Sabbath day and keep it holy.
5. Honor your father and mother.
6. You shall not murder.
7. You shall not commit adultery.
8. You shall not steal.
9. You shall not bear false witness against your neighbor.
10. You shall not covet anything that belongs to your neighbor.

These standards, if everyone would live by them, could transform our society as no government in history has ever been able to do. The very absolutes that are so detested by a humanistic, relativistic society would bring about the changes that same society is so desperately seeking.

Adherence to the first two commandments would eliminate the destruction that comes from worshiping *things* instead of the God who made us. Cheating, greed, and unethical business practices would disappear. Imagine the relationship we could have with God if we stopped worshiping things! In 1994 Pope John Paul II came to Denver to celebrate World Youth Day. Catholic kids were ecstatic to be able to catch a glimpse of the leader of their church. The media dubbed him "The Keeper of the Faith." Imagine how rich our lives would be if we sensed the presence of the *Author and Finisher* of our faith and worshiped him every day. Instead we choose to worship the impotent idols of materialism and self, whose only power is that they keep us from experiencing the real thing.

Imagine a world without profanity. The disrespect shown to God by taking his name in vain opens the door for the pollution of our entire language. Today men and women yell obscenities at each other, excusing themselves by saying that those words no longer mean what they used to mean. Yes, they do. We have just grown insensitive to their meaning in the same way that we have grown insensitive to the majesty and power of Almighty God.

Imagine the beauty of a day set aside for worship, rest, and contemplation of God's goodness. Even the Creator rested after six days of productivity. I wonder how many lives might be made richer—even lengthened—if one day a week were set aside as "the Lord's Day," as God intended. Stress, after all, is a great ruiner of lives. Rest and meditation alleviate stress.

What heartache and misery could be avoided if the youth of our nation would simply honor their fathers and mothers! Gangs would disintegrate for lack of membership. Detention centers would empty. Much of the chaos and violence we see in our youth culture would disappear.

Can you imagine living in a world without murder or adultery or stealing? Divorce rates would plummet. Newscasters would be at a loss for material. The tabloid presses would grind to a halt. The results would be astounding.

Of course, mankind has already proven that we are incapable of living up to these principles, which represent God's ideal. That's why Jesus came. But your personal world *can* be guided by these principles, which are defined in even more practical detail in much of the rest of Scripture. One of the reasons that God gave the law to the Israelites was to show them how incapable they were of living up to his perfect standard. They were unable to live according to the law, and that revealed to them how much they needed his supernatural intervention if they were to ever come even close to the potential he intended for them. God's law still represents his ideal. And the principles inherent in that law are invaluable to those who seek to fire up their lives.

Here's a suggestion: Write those commandments on a card and refer to them often. Post them at your desk, on your refrigerator—anywhere they will catch your eye. They are designed to keep you free, as these Scriptures suggest:

> All Scripture is God-breathed and is useful for teaching, rebuking, correcting and training in righteousness, so that the man of God may be thoroughly equipped for every good work. (2 Timothy 3:16–17)

> Blessed is the man who does not walk in the counsel of the wicked or stand in the way of sinners or sit in the seat of mockers. But his delight is in the law of the LORD, and on his law he meditates day and night. He is like a tree planted by streams of water, which yields its fruit in season and whose leaf does not wither. *Whatever he does prospers.* (Psalm 1:1–3, emphasis added)

It is not only the specific principles explicitly quoted from Scripture that will keep us on track in our personal call to excellence. We can also distill additional principles and values from Scripture by applying God's Word to our modern age and to our lives. In his book *Hide or Seek,* James Dobson identifies some of these values:

> But what does God value? We cannot substitute his system for ours unless we know what he has personally ordained. Fortunately, the Bible provides the key to God's value system for mankind In my judgment, it is composed of six all-important principles. They are:
>
> 1. Devotion to God
> 2. Love for mankind
> 3. Respect for authority
> 4. Obedience to divine commandments
> 5. Self-discipline and self-control
> 6. Humbleness of spirit
>
> These six concepts are from the hand of the Creator himself and are absolutely valid and relevant for our lives.[8]

Common sense, responsible corporate policy, loving family relationships, personal ethics, matters of conscience—all of these things are the result of following the principles of a godly life as presented in Scripture. It is useful to write these Scriptural principles out in general terms applicable to all areas of our lives, such as: *I will do everything in my power to keep my word.*

What effect will living by a principle such as this have on my life? It will cause me to carefully weigh any commitment I make in light of my ability to keep my promise. It will affect my purchasing decisions—if I'm not sure I can pay, I don't buy. It will affect the way I respond to my family—if I promise to set aside time for my children, that time will take priority.

Here's another example of a reworded biblical principle that would have a profound effect on my behavior: *I will avoid actions that would bring shame to my Lord, my family, or my friends.*

Oh, the pain and destruction that could be avoided if men and women would live by *that* one!

Are you feeling guilty because you already know you've failed to live by biblical principles? Don't give up. I have grievously breached some of the principles I have set for my personal life. Those times of failure will come for all of us. But that's no reason to give up. Yes, you will fail. And when you do, it's essential to accept God's forgiveness and claim his power to get back on track as soon as possible.

So then, the first step in identifying the principles that will guide your life is to examine God's Word, to make it a practical "user's manual" for your life. Make Scripture reading a part of your everyday routine. You'll be amazed at how many principles and guidelines you'll find there. Start a list! It will grow quickly. Remember, *principled people are powerful people.* To the degree that you allow God's Spirit to empower you to live by his Word, you will experience the fullness he intended for your life.

His love for you is not dependent on your adherence to these principles—*but your quality of life is.*

Unifying Principles

Unifying principles are the principles you choose in order to keep yourself focused on the specific purpose you have set for your life. It's too easy to rush through life by moving in several directions at once, choosing the *good* things (or maybe the *easy* things) rather than the *best* things. When you've identified your life's purpose, you'll want to focus your efforts and attitudes to accomplish that purpose, rather than wasting your efforts on other, less worthy pursuits. How do you choose those principles? By asking yourself, "What is consistent with my purpose for living and my personal fulfillment of that purpose?" The business-woman who feels called to glorify God in all aspects of her business, for instance, will establish specific business principles that protect the dignity of her customers and employees.

I established the unifying principles that guide our business in that same way. I believe that God uniquely equipped me to help people develop to the full potential for which they were created. That phrase is written right into my purpose statement. Any principle or activity that doesn't keep me focused on that purpose is questionable for me. For example, although I enjoy playing golf for relaxation, for me to spend most of my time on the golf course would distract me from the main focus of my life. On the other hand, there are some very gifted athletes who spend hours refining their skills on the golf course or in the gym, because using their athletic ability to the glory of God is part of their purpose for living.

The book of Hebrews mentions those things that can lead us away from God's calling for our life: "Therefore, since we are surrounded by such a great cloud of witnesses, let us throw off *everything that hinders* and the sin that so easily entangles, and let us run with perseverance the race marked out for us" (Hebrews 12:1, emphasis added).

It's not just that we need to avoid blatant sin. If we're to finish the race marked out for us, that verse from Hebrews tells us to throw off *everything that hinders* us from that race. Things that in and of themselves may not be sin can *become* sin, because they detour us from what God intended and hinder us from living to our fullest potential.

Here's an example: Suppose a minister determines that his purpose is to serve his congregation by demonstrating the love of Christ to the best of his ability. A couple of years later he finds himself working instead to build the biggest, most influential church in the United States. That lack of unity in his life will rob him of power and effectiveness. Trying to ignore the incongruity will drive him crazy. Trying to accomplish both will drive everyone around him crazy. That minister is badly in need of establishing some strict unifying principles in his life and sticking to them.

Time to create your own unifying principles. You established a purpose for your life back on page 56. Now rewrite that purpose in the appropriate place on the following page and then create a list of unifying principles that will keep you focused on that purpose. If you keep that list handy and review it regularly, you'll find yourself refining it over the years, as well as adding to it. Make this a lifelong process.

My Unifying Principles

I have established the following purpose for my life:

_____

_____

_____

In order to focus my life on that purpose, I resolve to live by the following principles:

_____

_____

_____

_____

_____

The Steps That Get You There

The third and final step toward maximum living is to plan the *steps* that will help you accomplish your purpose in life. As shown in figure 3, these are

Figure 3

the rungs of the ladder, bounded by the principles you have established and leading directly to your purpose for living.

Together these steps make up a plan that can include everything from the *big* things—aiming for a career or choosing a mate—to the   small details of everyday life. Your plan—your *goals*—pull these details together in a way that is consistent with your ultimate purpose and the principles you have set for living.

If you're a goal-driven person, you've probably been waiting (impatiently) for me to get to the part about setting goals. Well, we're there. I'm convinced, as you are, that goals are a powerful tool. But they are most powerful when they are guided by principles and focused to fulfill a purpose. Motivational speaker and author Charlie "Tremendous" Jones tells of a frenzied, haggard businessman running up to an airline counter and demanding a ticket. The agent asked, "Where are you going?" The businessman replied, "Just give me a ticket—I've got business everywhere." This man may have business *everywhere,* but he isn't going *anywhere* until he sets a goal to go *somewhere.*

Purpose must be balanced with *plan.* No matter how noble your purpose, without planned goals you won't accomplish it.

Imagine that, as you walk the paths of a beautiful forest, you come upon a man gazing up at the highest pinnacle of a majestic mountain. He is crying in despair. When you ask him why, he replies, "My whole purpose in life is to stand on that pinnacle. But in all the years in which I've held that purpose, I've never gotten any closer to it than I am right now."

"How long have you been standing here?" you ask him.

"I've been standing in this same spot for years," he answers.

What would you say to such a man? I know what I would tell him: "Start walking!" That man obviously doesn't understand that he will never experience the joy of standing on the summit (his ultimate purpose) until he crosses the stream in front of him, walks around the raspberry thicket, walks through the cedar grove beyond that, and accomplishes each of the thousand other small and attainable goals that will eventually take him where he wants to be. If goals without a purpose is like seed on a rock, then a purpose without goals is like a cultivated field without any seed at all.

In this chapter, you established your purpose for living and carefully chose the guidelines that will keep you on track. Keeping that purpose and your guiding principles in mind, you are now able to set the goals that will lead you to abundant living.

Notice, however, that I have not provided in this chapter a place to write those goals. That's because I believe they should be recorded in your appointment book or someplace else where you'll have the opportunity to review them often. List both short-term and long-term goals. Identify the immediate steps necessary to accomplish those goals, and record those steps on a "to do" list. Set a specific time to take action on those steps. Then *do it*. You now know where you're going and how you're going to get there. It's time for action!

So start walking. Break into a jog. Leap. Begin to enjoy the freedom that comes from directed living. Of course you'll stumble from time to time, and sometimes you'll fall flat on your face. But the course is set. There's no turning back. It's time to run.

---

1. Robert F. Mager, *Developing Attitude Toward Learning* (Belmont, Calif.: Fearon-Pitman, 1968; Lake Publishing, 1984), vii.
2. Friedrich Nietzsche, *Twilight of the Idols: The Anti-Christ*, trans. R. J. Holingdale (New York: Penguin, 1968), 23.
3. Steven R. Covey, *The Seven Habits of Highly Effective People* (New York: Simon & Schuster, 1989), 98–99.
4. John W. Alexander, *Managing Our Work*, rev. (Downers Grove, Ill.: Inter-Varsity Press, 1975), 19.
5. Ted Engstrom and Edward R. Dayton, *The Art of Management for Christian Leaders* (Waco, Tex.: Word, 1976), 19.
6. Viktor E. Frankl, *Man's Search for Meaning*, 3d ed. rev., trans. Ilse Lasch (New York: Simon & Schuster, 1984), 81–82.
7. Vernard Eller, *The Mad Morality* (Nashville: Abingdon, 1970), 8.
8. James Dobson, *Hide or Seek* (Old Tappan, N.J.: Revell, 1974), 158.

Chapter 4
WHAT DOES GOD WANT?

The whole problem of guidance, after all, is to know how the Holy Spirit guides—what means he has chosen to use—and my contention is that he has never promised to lead us by inward convictions but only by wisdom, judgment, and advice based upon knowledge of and obedience to the Scriptures.[1]

If we agree that God's *intention* for our lives and *living our lives to the fullest* are one and the same, then finding out God's purpose for our lives becomes of extreme importance. In theological jargon, the question is, How can we know God's will for our lives? Is his "will" some cosmic secret he wants us to spend a lifetime trying to discover, or are there steps we can take to be reasonably sure we're on the right track?

I often watch adults and teenagers struggle to know the will of God. For them each of life's decisions becomes a point of confusion. These people are paralyzed. "Is this God's will—or my *own* will?" they lament as they try to choose a career, a college, or a church. Because they don't know exactly what God wants them to do, they're afraid to do anything. It's appropriate to be concerned about doing the "right thing"—but the uncertainty and indecision faced by so many over everyday decisions is not appropriate, nor is it helpful.

In the Old Testament (Judges 6:36–40), Gideon tested the will of God by laying a fleece on the ground.

"If you will save Israel by my hand as you have promised," Gideon said, "in the morning, cover the fleece with dew and let the ground around it be dry."

Gideon knew that what he asked was, naturally speaking, impossible. Therefore if it happened, he would know that he had received a sign from God. Even so, when he found the fleece soaked and the ground around it dry the next morning, he still wasn't sure.

"Don't be angry with me," he said to God. "Let me make one more request. Allow me one more test with the fleece. If you really want to use my hand to save Israel, this time make the fleece be dry and all the ground covered with dew."

Fortunately for Gideon, God was patient. The next morning, Gideon found the fleece dry and the ground wet, just as he had requested.

Reluctance to act on what God reveals as his will (particularly if it requires risk or discomfort) causes many modern-day seekers to try the fleece method to find God's will. Sometimes they lay out so many fleeces that they forget which one belongs to which problem. At other times, they're tempted to slant the test to confirm their own inclinations. "Fleecing" doesn't produce confirmed decisions—it produces naked sheep.

In the words of Philip Yancey, "'Putting out the fleece' hardly seems an appropriate model for someone seeking guidance; it better describes someone who knows exactly what God wants and still quakes before the task."[2]

Once, before getting on a bus, I prayed silently, "Dear God, if you want me to talk to someone today about your love, please give me a sign." How silly! The Bible is full of directives to share God's love with those around us. That should have been all the "sign" I needed. A better prayer would have been, "Give me the courage to share my faith today whenever the opportunity arises."

As with Gideon, God was patient and played the fleece game with me. I had just seated myself comfortably when a young businessman sat down next to me. After a moment, to my surprise, he began to cry—first quietly, just a few tears running down his cheeks, but soon his emotions overwhelmed him, and he began to weep uncontrollably. When he regained his composure, he turned to me and apologized, explaining that his life was a mess and that he had no hope of cleaning it up. "If only I knew God," he sighed. Then, looking directly at me, he asked, "Do *you* know God?"

What more of a sign could I want? This fleece was dripping with confirmation. But I was too chicken to take action. I wanted more proof. *Dear God,* I silently prayed, *is this a sign?* Of course it was sign! What was I going to pray next? *Lord, if this is a sign, turn the bus driver into an armadillo?* Unfortunately, even when we know what God wants, we often look for a test that will excuse us from acting on that knowledge.

So that we could know his will, God gave us the Bible—along with a mind capable of reason, which he expects us to use. Despite our God-given ability to reason, we sometimes wish the Bible would reason for us, relieving us of the responsibility of making personal decisions. The Word of God gives very clear guidance on some questions. A man or woman contemplating an extramarital affair won't need to read far to discover God's will concerning that behavior. But in other areas, the Bible has little or nothing specific to say. Should you take that scuba diving vacation? Should you accept that new job offer, even though you'd have to move? The Bible won't give you specific, yes-or-no answers to those questions.

So then, if God's will is our blueprint for maximum living, and if the Bible doesn't give us specific instructions on what God's will is for many of the day-to-day decisions we must make, how do we find God's will in those matters—imitate Gideon and lay out a fleece?

Paul answers that question in a letter he wrote to the Christians in Rome. He doesn't suggest that you skin any sheep, start laying out fleeces, or ask God to change bus drivers into strange animals. Instead he gives clear directions for testing God's will. After listing those directions, Paul reveals one of the key steps to living life with the gusto that God intended. First, let's look at some misconceptions about the will of God. Then let's list and evaluate our resources for knowing his will. Finally, we'll review the instructions Paul gave for discovering God's perfect will.

What Is God's Will?

One of the reasons we're so confused about finding God's will is that we have so many misconceptions about his will and about how he reveals it to us. Those misconceptions keep us from seeing the truth. Let's look at some of the more common ones.

Misconception 1: God's Will Is Always Something I Will Hate

As a teenager, I was afraid to entrust God with my life. I thought he would send me someplace where there would be snakes, spiders, and naked people who eat other people. God's will, I figured, had to be something I would hate.

I didn't even want to think about the kind of woman he had in mind for me. I was sure that ugliness, wrinkles, and hair pulled severely back into a bun would be part of the picture. Certainly God would never give me somebody appealing and sweet. I was wrong on all counts. God has blessed me with a wonderful wife. She's not only beautiful and intelligent; for twenty-five years she has also demonstrated the courage to stay with a wrinkled man who doesn't have enough hair left to put into a bun.

"God's will" comes closer to meeting the deepest desires of our hearts than we imagine. But don't misunderstand—that is *not* to say that God's will is always without sacrifice or pain.

Trouble should always be treated as a call to consider one's ways. But trouble is not necessarily a sign of being off track at all: for as the Bible declares in general that "many are the afflictions of the righteous" (Psalm 34:19 NRSV), so it teaches in particular that following God's guidance regularly leads to upsets and distresses that we would otherwise have escaped.[3]

Some of the most contented people I know have followed God to places where there are snakes, spiders, and people who eat people. But they wouldn't trade their difficult lifestyles for any of the comforts you and I enjoy. We can learn a valuable truth from these dedicated servants of God. Even when God leads you through difficult times, you won't find a more fulfilling life than the one you can live right in the center of God's will.

Misconception 2: I've Already Missed My Chance at God's Will

This paralyzing misconception springs from Satan's lie that once you have sinned, you'll forever have to settle for God's second best. Because of your sin, you'll never be in the right place at the right time—like you could have been if you hadn't messed up. It's too late for you now. You've already married the wrong person or gone to the wrong school or committed a socially gross sin, the stigma of which will follow you for the rest of your life. Don't even *think* about moving into a prime position of ministry. You're not worthy.

Those who preach this misconception (and there are many) hasten to assure you that God can still use you—but only in an inferior capacity. "The assumption is that God lacks either the will or the wisdom or both to get you back on track; therefore a substandard spiritual life is all that is open to you now."[4]

The first time I heard this lie, it was spoken by someone counseling a teenage girl who had just had a baby outside of marriage. "Because of what you have done," he said, "you will always have to settle for God's second best."

What a terrible thought! Yes, it's true that we have messed up the original beauty of God's creation. We live in a fallen world—God's second best, if you will. But has this young lady sinned so much more than the rest of us that she'll have to settle for second best while the counselor and you and I can step up and claim God's first and best and perfect will for ourselves? No, if we're to apply that counselor's reasoning logically, we've *all* sinned seriously enough to disqualify us from God's perfect will, and we'll *all* have to settle for second best. *None* of us can experience God's will. In fact, if that counselor is right, the words "seeking God's will" are ludicrous.

If sinning removes us forever from the possibility of knowing God's will, then why even try? For a very good reason: God's will is available to sinners. The Bible tells us to seek his will—why would it say that if we had no hope of ever participating in his will? Here's the good news: We are saved by God's grace, our sins are wiped out, and he still has a good and perfect will in mind for us.

Are we minimizing sin by this approach? What happens when one has indeed made a bad mistake?

> Is the damage irrevocable? Must they now be put off course for life? Thank God, no. Our God is a God who not merely restores but takes up our mistakes and follies into his plan for us and brings good out of them. This is a part of his gracious sovereignty.[5]

Will that young unmarried girl face consequences for her actions? Undoubtedly, as will the boy who fathered her child, the counselor who counseled her, and all of the rest of us who have been guilty of sin. But those consequences do not mean banishment from God's will. If you jump from a three-story building, you probably won't run a marathon the next day. But I doubt that you would blame God. You would know that your broken bones, bruises, and sprains were the result of a poor choice of your own.

When you point to a hot stove and tell your child, "Don't touch," you are trying to help your child avoid some painful consequences. If your child ignores the warning and touches the hot stove, he will be burned. Is that burn the punishment you gave your child for his disobedience? No. It is a *consequence* of his disobedience. The beautiful thing about knowing Christ and experiencing his forgiveness is that God makes it possible for us to find and obey his will in spite of our sinful nature—and even in the midst of the consequences of that sin.

God's will is like the current in a river; it is always there. As you spin out of control in some eddy, he is waiting. When you finally make up your mind to seek his forgiveness and to trust him, you can slip back into the stream and be caught up in the current again, right in the center of his will. Did you waste time and miss opportunities as you spun out of control? Yes. But once God puts you back in the center of his will, you'll have new opportunities. Paul said, "Forgetting what is behind and straining toward what is ahead, I press on toward the goal to win the prize for which God has called me heavenward in Christ Jesus" (Philippians 3:13–14).

I explain this misconception at such length because I have met so many adults who have put themselves on the shelf because of past sin or missed opportunity, believing they have lost any chance they had to be a part of God's will. I'll say it again: that is *Satan's lie*. God wants to direct your life by starting from whatever situation you find yourself in at this minute, regardless of what mistakes you may have made in the past. Paul says that God will bring good from even your most difficult circumstances and lead you closer to his original purpose for your life. "And we know that in all things God works for the good of those who love him, who have been called according to his purpose" (Romans 8:28).

No matter what you've done, God wants you back in the mainstream of his will.

Misconception 3: God's Will Is Whatever I Think It Should Be

God's will is not simply a matter of opinion. It would certainly be convenient if it were, though, wouldn't it? That way, we could do whatever we wanted to do and call it God's will—a great way to give credibility to our own desires. And that, unfortunately, is the way many people approach God's will. A girlfriend once explained to me that God had told her she should break up with me. How could I argue with her? I'd have been arguing with God! She went on to say, in essence, that God had told her I wasn't good enough for her. (That did a lot for my self-esteem.) The truth was, she didn't want to go out with me anymore and didn't want to be the one to tell me. So she had God tell me. That way she didn't have to be responsible for her own actions.

It's easy to justify an action by saying it's God's will. But his will is not something we make up; it isn't based simply on what we want or how we would like things to be. It's *God's* will, not ours. It's more than an opinion—it's a plan. It's God's plan. Let's look at the ways in which he reveals that plan to you and me.

May the Source Be with You

You don't find God's will by looking in the want ads, an advice column, or a horoscope. You can't even go to your friends or a counselor to discover God's will (although their advice can help point you in the right direction). Three sources reveal God's will.

The Bible: God's Will in Black and White

Most of what you can know of God's will is found in his book. The Bible spells out very specifically what your relationship with God was meant to be, how you should treat other people, and what criteria to use in making everyday decisions. For instance, there is no reason to agonize over what method you should use to get revenge on someone who has wronged you. The Bible clearly directs you to treat even your enemies with love. In many of our daily decisions, in many of our questions concerning God's will, the Bible's instructions are clear.

But the Bible isn't a fortune cookie. It doesn't provide specific instructions about every situation, and it can be misunderstood and misused. A man who faced financial difficulties went to the Bible to find a specific course of action. He opened the Bible at random, closed his eyes, and jabbed his finger down on the page. When he opened his eyes, he was horrified to read, "So Judas threw the money into the temple and left. Then he went away and hanged himself" (Matthew 27:5). *There must be some mistake,* he thought. So he closed his eyes and took another stab at it. This time, his finger fell on Luke 10:37: "Go and do likewise." Shaken, he decided to give it one last try. With eyes closed tightly, he turned several pages and then allowed his finger to land once more. He opened his eyes and read, "What you are about to do, do quickly" (John 13:27).

Needless to say, he looked elsewhere for advice.

That man could have found guidance for his particular situation in the Bible *if he'd known how to look for such guidance and how to recognize it when he found it.* The Bible doesn't directly address every situation we encounter in life. Even so, in those situations that the Bible doesn't directly address, its guidelines are sufficient to point you in the right direction. That's why the Bible is the main source for the universal principles discussed in the previous chapter.

Principles is the key word here. When you face difficult daily decisions—and even the bigger decisions, like a career change—you'll search the Bible in vain for a specific answer. Nor should you expect God to light up a huge, celestial neon sign that says "Go with IBM" or "Search for a tall, dark stranger." Instead God's guidance comes in the form of biblical principles. In deciding how to apply those principles, God expects you to use the brain he installed during your assembly.

Just how do you do that? When you're searching for a job, for instance, how do you apply biblical principles? R. C. Sproul suggests answers to the following questions:

1.   What can I do?

> Make a sober analysis of yourself.
> Take proficiency tests and evaluations: check your skills
>   and abilities.
> Take aptitude tests which determine your latent and
>   acquired abilities.

2.   What should I do?

> The most practical advice I can give . . . is for you to do
>   what your motivated ability pattern indicates you can
>   do with a high degree of motivation.
> Keeping in mind, of course, God's precepts.[6]

Or how about the question, Whom should I marry? Does God have one person picked out for you? Does he then assign you the job of finding that person among the millions on the face of the earth? Or does he want you to follow Scripture's guidelines for choosing a mate and then trust him to lead you to the right kind of person?

The Christians in Corinth faced this question. Look at Paul's response: "A woman is bound to her husband as long as he lives. But if her husband dies, she is free to marry anyone she wishes, but he must belong to the Lord" (1 Corinthians 7:39). Paul didn't say that the widow had to find some mystery person chosen by

God. Instead he established a guideline: she was to marry someone who belonged to the Lord. Within that guideline, she was free to make a choice.

Imagine Adam and Eve eating the "First Supper." God has told them, "From any tree of the garden you may eat freely, but from the tree of the knowledge of good and evil you shall not eat." Adam asks Eve to make supper. Eve wants to cook according to the Lord's will. She asks Adam to seek the Lord to find out what he wants them to eat. Adam finds God, and the Lord repeats, "From any tree of the garden...." This happens a couple of times until Adam and Eve finally get the message. They are free to choose within the limits of the guidelines that God has given them; in this case, they can eat anything in the garden—except for the fruit of one tree.

> The principle of freedom of choice within revealed limits was clearly part of the Creator's design from the very beginning. And it is a principle that continues to be applied routinely in everyday situations.[7]

Here's another clear biblical principle—the importance of seeking the counsel and advice of others: "The way of a fool seems right to him, but a wise man listens to advice" (Proverbs 12:15). According to J. I. Packer, "It is a sign of conceit and immaturity to ignore advice in major decisions."[8]

It would be great, when we're facing a difficult life-decision, to hear a voice from heaven directing us to a specific course of action. But don't we have that? When handled properly, the Bible is our "voice from heaven." It is God's Word to us. It should be studied diligently for what it says about the way God wants us to live. It is *the* major source of knowing God's will.

> God enables us to discern [his will] by prayerfully using our minds—thinking how Scripture applies, comparing alternatives, weighing advice, taking account of our heart's desire, estimating what we are capable of. Some might call

this common sense, but the Bible calls it wisdom, and sees it as one of God's most precious gifts.[9]

One word of caution. Don't expect God to lay out, in one huge blueprint, the plan for the rest of your life. That isn't the way he works. He will give you the wisdom you need—one step at a time. And that, after all, is best; we would never be able to handle such a long view into the future.

Natural Law: If You Trip, It Is God's Will That You Fall Down

Natural law is a part of God's will. I am always amazed when I meet Christians who mistakenly believe that they are exempt from this aspect of God's will. Sometimes they seem to expect God's will to be contrary to the natural laws that he established. When God created this world, he put certain natural laws into place as a part of his will. He created our bodies and our world to work according to those laws. If you intentionally mistreat your body with poor health habits, it is part of God's natural law—his will—that you suffer the consequences of that treatment. If you take a sharp curve at one hundred miles per hour, the law of centrifugal force (God's will) will cause your car to leave the road. Rather than *fire up* your life, a decision like that could *douse* the fire in your life.

I once counseled a young man who was sexually involved with his girlfriend. "I pray constantly that she won't get pregnant," he said.

"I'm going to be straight with you," I replied. "Listen up. If you keep sleeping with your girlfriend, she *is* going to get pregnant. That's the way God created the world; why would he change it for you?"

That young man was sowing wild oats and praying for crop failure. The laws that govern nature *are* God's will. We must not assume that because we are Christians, we can defy those laws and expect him to intercede. If a Christian and a non-Christian jump from the Empire State Building at the same time, they'll both hit the ground at the same time. And just as hard. The natural laws that govern this universe are universal.

Why bring this up? Because if you really seek to live life to its fullest, you can't ignore this important part of God's will. Whether you are trying to prove your worth by attempting to be something other than what you were created to be, or whether you are fighting God's laws because you think you have a spiritual exemption, you are wasting time and energy. As you seek to make the right decisions daily, don't expect God to break his own natural laws on your behalf.

The Holy Spirit: Your Personal Guide in the Quest

> But the Counselor, the Holy Spirit, whom the Father will send in my name, will teach you all things and will remind you of everything I have said to you. (John 14:26)

> But when he, the Spirit of truth, comes, he will guide you into all truth. He will not speak on his own; he will speak only what he hears, and he will tell you what is yet to come. He will bring glory to me by taking from what is mine and making it known to you. (John 16:13–14)

God reveals his will to you as the Holy Spirit touches your heart and mind to move you to action. Philippians 2:13 encourages us: "For it is God who works in you to will and to act according to his good purpose." But because the Holy Spirit doesn't send his messages with a return address, it can be difficult to discern whether what we are hearing and feeling is his prompting or some other influence. That's why it is always important to carefully examine what you believe the Holy Spirit is encouraging you to do, and to check it against the Bible for confirmation. If you don't, and if your mind and heart aren't firmly anchored in the truth of God's Word, you may follow other influences and motivations and attribute those to the Holy Spirit.

All impressions must be rigorously tested by appeal to biblical wisdom—the corporate wisdom of the believing community, be it said, as well as any personal wisdom one has—lest impressions that are rooted in egoism, pride, headstrong unrealism, a fancy that irrationality glorifies God, a sense that some human being is infallible, or any similar unhealthiness of soul, be allowed to masquerade as Spirit-given. Only impressions verified as biblically appropriate and practically wise should be treated as coming from God.[10]

Giving us the ability to recognize the voice of the Holy Spirit is one of the most powerful ways God has of guiding us to maximum living. That's why we should do the following:

1. Avoid the misconceptions discussed earlier in this chapter.
2. Study God's Word with a mind and heart open to obedience.
3. Respect the natural laws that God has put in place.
4. Seek wise advice.
5. Use the brains that God has given us.

Now that we've looked at the primary resources that God has provided for us so we may discern his will, let's look at Paul's specific direction for identifying God's will.

Paul's Formula for Maximum Living

Give God Your Body

According to Paul's great passage on finding God's will (Romans 12:1–2), the first step toward knowing the will of God is to give God your body.

> Therefore, I urge you, brothers, in view of God's mercy, to offer your bodies as living sacrifices, holy and pleasing to God—this is your spiritual act of worship (Romans 12:1).

Do you remember when I said in chapter 1 that the greatest expression of worship is to be everything God created you to be? That process begins by giving back to him everything he has given to you. Unless your body belongs to God, you will never be confident of what he wants for your life.

That sounds simple—but it's neither simple nor easy. You rarely hear, in testimonies or even sermons, people offering their bodies as living sacrifices. It's easier to talk about committing your *life* to God. That's vague enough that it doesn't hurt much. Giving God your body is more difficult. It's much more specific. We care very much about our bodies. Even so, our bodies are exactly what God wants. The whole thing: hands, feet, lips, intellect, sexuality, eyes—even that receding hairline. He wants it all, offered to him of our own free will as a living sacrifice.

Little children express the reality of this in a song. The verses are:

> Oh, be careful little hands what you do.
> Oh, be careful little feet where you go.
> Oh, be careful little eyes what you see.

And the chorus of this beautiful little song concludes:

> For the Father up above is looking down in love,
> So be careful little hands what you do.

The person who penned those words must have read Romans. That is the kind of commitment that Paul is talking about:

> Do not offer the parts of your body to sin, as instruments of wickedness, but rather offer yourselves to God, as those who have been brought from death to life; and offer the parts of your body to him as instruments of righteousness.... Don't you know that ... you are slaves to the one whom you obey— whether you are slaves to sin, which leads to death, or to obedience, which leads to righteousness? (Romans 6:13, 16)

There are only two options. One leads to abundant life, and the other leads to death.

What does this have to do with knowing God's will? Imagine how our lives would change if we were constantly aware that our bodies belonged to God. Imagine walking through the next workday while singing to yourself, "Oh, be careful little lips what you say. . . ." I know it sounds crazy. (It'll sound even crazier to the people around you, so be sure to sing it to yourself.) As you sing, you would be constantly aware that your lips belong to God. The first time you were about to hurt someone with cruel words or were tempted to tell a lie or were starting to share a juicy piece of gossip, you would immediately remember that those are God's lips. They were not designed for telling lies or hurting people. Let's face it—sometimes we go for weeks without thinking about who designed our body and about what he wants us to do with it. We miss out on gusto living for this reason, among others. We may consider what God wants when dealing with the *big* decisions—but unless we are giving him our lips and arms and minds minute by minute, allowing him to control our bodies in the little actions of everyday life, we will not be prepared to know what he wants when the bigger decisions come our way.

The more you give him every little part of yourself, the more sensitive you become to what he wants. Have you unconditionally surrendered your body to the Savior? If not, now would be an excellent time. It's the first step toward knowing his will.

Give God Your Will

The second step is to give God your will. That means making up your mind that more than anything else, you want what he wants. Instead of allowing your own desires or the pressure of your world to run your life, you make the commitment that only God will run it.

Paul puts it this way: "Do not conform any longer to the pattern of this world" (Romans 12:2). The Phillips version of the New Testament puts that verse more graphically: "Don't let the world press you into its mold." If you're letting the "mold" of the world (pun intended) be the guiding influence in your decision making, you're going to have a terrible time figuring out what God wants for your life. If Jesus hadn't been totally committed to doing the will of the Father, we would be without hope today. But when all the pressures around him screamed that he should run and avoid the pain and humiliation of the cross, he prayed, "Yet not as I will, but as you will" (Matthew 26:39). His decision to go to the cross was not the easy decision, but he knew it was the right decision.

Who really owns your will? Is it your business associates? Your friends? Is it the circumstances of everyday life? Your church? Or is it God? He wants nothing less than your total commitment to allow him to direct your life to the ultimate potential for which you were designed. If you are willing to make that commitment, he'll be able to show you what he wants. In fact, he'll work within you to change the very source of your desires so that they are in sync with his desires.

Give God Your Mind

To know God's will, your commitment to avoid being pressured into the world's mold must be accompanied by a third step: give God your mind.

> Do not conform any longer to the pattern of this world, but be transformed by the renewing of your mind. (Romans 12:2)

God wants your mind. An ad on television says, "A mind is a terrible thing to waste." How true! And a mind that is not given to God *is* wasted, no matter how accomplished its owner seems to be. The only way we can avoid conformity to this world is to transform our minds—to make sure that their thought processes are controlled and influenced by his Word rather than by the random and evil directions of this world. That's why regular Bible reading is so important.

A prescription for transforming your mind is found in a passage we looked at earlier, from the book of Psalms:

> Blessed is the man who does not walk in the counsel of the wicked or stand in the way of sinners or sit in the seat of mockers. But his delight is in the law of the LORD, and on his law he meditates day and night. He is like a tree planted by streams of water, which yields its fruit in season and whose leaf does not wither. Whatever he does prospers. (Psalm 1:1–3)

God reveals, in these verses, two requirements for transforming your mind. Let's examine them.

1. Put a Guard at the Gate

Psalm 1:1 suggests that we avoid the influence of evil people. That doesn't mean that we shouldn't love or associate with unbelievers. It *does* mean that we should refuse to be influenced by ungodly thinking. Don't seek counsel from those who don't trust Christ. To do so is to risk letting thought patterns that are not centered on serving and following God control your mind. "The sinful mind is hostile to God. It does not submit to God's law, nor can it do so" (Romans 8:7).

Genghis Khan swept across China and Mongolia, conquering everything in his path. Many of the cities he conquered had huge armies and were fortified by immense walls, yet he managed to overcome them. When asked how he managed to get past the great protecting walls of those cities, he simply responded, "We bribed the gatekeeper." All he had to do was get past the person who guarded the gate, and the city was easy pickings.

Your mind is the gate to your soul. If it can be compromised, your soul will crumble. Listen to how Paul pleads with the Corinthians in this regard:

> I beg you that when I come I may not have to be as bold as I expect to be toward some people who think that we live by the standards of this world. For though we live in the world, we do not wage war as the world does. The weapons we fight with

are not the weapons of the world. On the contrary, they have divine power to demolish strongholds. We demolish arguments and every pretension that sets itself up against the knowledge of God, and we take captive every thought to make it obedient to Christ. (2 Corinthians 10:2–5)

According to that Scripture, Genghis Khan isn't the only one who uses the strategy of bribing the gatekeeper—Satan uses it, too. Only by controlling our thoughts and the influences on our minds can we withstand Satan's attacks. Unfortunately, few people have a guard of any kind at the gate to their mind. They allow every thought, idea, and image that comes along to enter their mind—and then wonder why they have a tough time knowing God's will. If you want to be sensitive to God's will, you must *transform your mind*. You must decide that some influences will not be allowed to cloud your thinking.

Several years ago my wife's parents were visiting our home. One evening we rented a video. The family sat down for an enjoyable evening at the movies. About fifteen minutes into the video, I could tell that my father-in-law was uncomfortable. Finally he could keep silent no longer. "How can you allow this trash into your home?" he exclaimed.

At first I was defensive. After all, the movie was rated PG. But I knew that my father-in-law was not one to interfere in people's lives and that, therefore, if he felt concerned enough to speak out like this, he must have felt that he had good reason. I could see genuine concern in his eyes.

"Would you allow a guest in your living room to use that language or act out what we are watching?" he continued.

"Of course not," I answered, still somewhat defensive.

"Ken," he said, "that's exactly what you *have* done. You've allowed these actors to come right into your living room to portray a lifestyle totally contrary to the values you have chosen to teach your children."

He was right. The enemy had sneaked right past the gate-keeper. That wasn't hard, because the gatekeeper to my mind had been asleep for some time.

It's unbelievable what we will allow into our homes and minds because it sneaks in as a part of the entertainment media. There are times when we should get up and leave the movie the-ater or turn off the TV or radio. If someone were insulting a per-son you love, you would either leave the room or tell that person to be quiet. Yet we don't give Christ that same courtesy. We watch casually, and sometimes join in the laughter, as the media blasphemes the One who gave his life for us.

Want to know God's will for your life? Want to live life to the maximum? Put a guard at the gate of your mind, and refuse to expose yourself to the destructive evil influences that so easily distort our view of his will. Why are we so careless about the media we expose ourselves to? Because we believe we're not influenced by what we watch. That isn't logical. The same people who tell us that the hours of sexually explicit lyrics in today's music and that the violence and moral decadence of the media have no appreciable influence on our lives are the people who spend millions of dollars on thirty-second commercials because they know that what we watch *will* influence us. Millions of bro-ken lives testify to the dangers of Satan's ability to influence the mind through the media, as well as through many other ways. Solomon said that what a person thinks is what he or she will become. Most psychologists agree.

The extremes of that influence lead to tragic lives—like that of serial killer Ted Bundy, a man who let the ever-increasing influence of pornography translate the unspeakable evil desires of his heart into action. Just as tragic, though, is the soul con-fused and cut off from knowing God's will by the influence of a deadly enemy that made it past the gate. We are vulnerable.

Guard your mind.

2. Renew Your Mind with Scripture

To transform your mind, you'll need more than just a bouncer to keep out any negative thoughts. The first psalm points out, in the second verse, another necessary step: "But his delight is in the law of the LORD, and on his law he meditates day and night."

People who want to know God's will immerse themselves in God's Word and find delight in discovering how God thinks and what God wants. That's why God can say: "Delight yourself in the LORD and he will give you the desires of your heart" (Psalm 37:4).

I once thought that this verse in Psalm 37 was a little strange. Could it possibly mean that if I delight myself in the law of the Lord, he will even grant my *dark and evil* desires? That's a false question! If I delight myself in his law, then I'll be delighted with the things that delight God. I'll be able to see through my dark and evil desires; I'll realize that they won't bring me the pleasure they promise and that they'll lead me down a destructive path—so they will *cease to be my desires*. Instead my desires will begin to fall more into line with what God intended for my life in the first place, and I'll be right on track to full-potential living.

Here are a couple of other verses that say the same thing: "Those who live in accordance with the Spirit have their minds set on what the Spirit desires" (Romans 8:5). "So I say, live by the Spirit, and you will not gratify the desires of the sinful nature" (Galatians 5:16).

If you delight yourself in things that are an abomination to God, then obviously those are the things you'll want. Do you see why the guard at your mind's door is so important? If you try to discover God's will while immersing yourself in the counsel of evil, how will you tell which is God's will and which is the influence of the Enemy? It's a recipe for confusion.

What does all of this have to do with gusto living? Look again at the entire passage from Psalm 1. The quality of life you're seeking is clearly identified there as a by-product of giving God your mind:

> Blessed is the man who does not walk in the counsel of the wicked or stand in the way of sinners or sit in the seat of mockers. But his delight is in the law of the LORD, and on his law he meditates day and night. He is like a tree planted by the streams of water, which yields its fruit in season and whose leaf does not wither. Whatever he does prospers. (Psalm 1:1–3)

So What?

Why does Paul beg the Roman Christians to give their bodies, wills, and minds to the Lord? Because that is the secret to knowing God's will. God doesn't require that you spend hours in fervent prayer, begging him to reveal his secrets to you. He doesn't want you to agonize over every decision you make. You don't have to spend months in doubt when deciding which car you should buy or whether you should make a career change. (Some cars require a career change just to pay for them.) You won't need to skin hundreds of sheep just so you can lay out their fleeces, nor will you need to make up other elaborate tests to find his will.

How, then, are we to know God's will? "The Bible contains very little specific advice on the techniques of guidance but very much on the proper way to maintain a love relationship with God."[11] A relationship with God is exactly what Paul is describing in Romans 12:1–2. Give your body to God without reservation. Give your will to God by refusing to be pushed around by the world and by committing yourself to whatever he wants for your life. And last, give your mind to God by putting a guard at the gate and saturating your mind with God's Word. Do this and God will have what he wants most. He does not want your adherence to a technique; he wants you—all of you. Body, mind, and will. Or as my father used to say, lock, stock, and barrel. God has already proved that he is committed to you. If you are committed to him, if your heart is intent on pleasing him, then because of your love for him, he will be a part of every decision you make. Trust him. He will faithfully show you when you are headed in the wrong direction.

Ask God for his help. As you seek his will in your life, pray, "Lord, I have carefully considered the alternatives in making this decision. You know my desire to do your will. Guide me and help me to stay dead center where you want me to be." Then don't second-guess him. Make your decision with confidence based on the facts that are available to you, and trust him.

Paul's instructions in Romans 12:1–2 end with this statement: "Then [after you've given God your body, refused to be compromised by the world, and transformed your mind] you will be able to test and approve what God's will is—his good, pleasing and perfect will."

Where do you find that gusto living for which your heart yearns? Right at the center of God's perfect will.

---

1. Oliver R. Barclay, *Guidance* (Downers Grove, Ill.: InterVarsity Press, 1978), 37. (First published by Inter-Varsity Press, Leicester, UK).
2. Philip Yancey, *Guidance* (Portland, Ore.: Multnomah Press, 1983), 4.
3. J. I. Packer, *Finding God's Will* (Downers Grove, Ill.: InterVarsity Press, 1985), 23.
4. J. I. Packer, "Wisdom Along the Way," *Eternity* (April 1986), 20.
5. Packer, *Finding God's Will*, 27.
6. R. C. Sproul, *God's Will and the Christian* (Wheaton, Ill.: Tyndale House, 1984), 62–63, 69.
7. Garry Friesen, *Decision Making and the Will of God* (Portland, Ore.: Multnomah Press, 1980), 167.
8. Packer, *Finding God's Will*, 19.
9. Packer, "Wisdom Along the Way," 23.
10. J. I. Packer, "True Guidance," *Eternity* (June 1986), 37.
11. Yancey, *Guidance*, 12.

Chapter 5

BERNIE KNOWS THE TRUTH

*Know the truth, and the truth will
set you free.*

—John 8:32

A s I mentioned earlier in this book, in my teens I lived to
prove my worth to those around me. Because of this, I often
misused the gifts God had given me. Humor is a gift from
God, a sword that can pierce through hostility and hardness to
reach even the coldest heart with a message of love. But I had
turned the other edge of the sword and used this gift to hurt
others.

And that is exactly what I did to a boy named Bernie one year
at church camp. Bernie was mentally and physically handi-
capped. He walked with a clumsy gait and talked with a slur.
Totally uninhibited and outgoing, Bernie sought the friendship
of everyone, but few of us had time for him.

For me Bernie was merely a source of material. I made jokes
about him and would mock his actions behind his back. Because
I was living with something to prove, I was willing to step on
Bernie in an attempt to lift myself a little higher.

One day on the athletic field, two captains were choosing
sides for a softball game, and Bernie and I were the last to be
chosen. I was humiliated. In that moment, I breathed a horribly
inappropriate prayer: "Please, God, let them choose me next." I

was chosen next, as it turned out, leaving Bernie standing alone. Bernie's eyes lit up—he didn't care about being chosen last; he only wanted to be chosen, and now that he was the only one left, surely it was his turn. But Bernie's look of anticipation quickly disappeared as the team captains began to argue about who would have to take him.

"You take him," one insisted.

"No, you take him," the other countered.

A counselor quickly stepped in and assigned Bernie to a team. Sadly, I was oblivious to the pain Bernie was probably feeling at that moment. I had avoided the embarrassment of being chosen last, and that was all I cared about; now we could get on with the game.

In fact, I probably wouldn't remember Bernie today if it weren't for what happened at the end of our stay at camp. It was time to go home, and everyone was standing by the buses, waiting to have their luggage loaded. I was with three boys who had become my friends during the week. Friends were a rare luxury for me, and I had compromised in many ways to gain the approval of these boys. As we stood saying our good-byes and promising to never lose contact (I can't even remember their names today), we heard Bernie coming, shouting at the top of his lungs, his voice cracking with excitement. "Good newth!" he cried with his familiar lisp. "Good newth!"

I quickly prepared to make my friends laugh one more time by mocking Bernie's cry, but before I could make that cruel response, Bernie broke into our circle.

His eyes danced with a joy I had not seen before. He gulped, catching his breath. "Good newth!" he breathed in a hoarse whisper. "*Jesuth* lovth me." Then, pointing to his heaving chest, he changed the emphasis. "Jesuth lovth *me!*" Bernie's eyes danced as, with arms outstretched to emphasize his point, he vigorously nodded his head up and down, waiting for us to acknowledge this newly discovered truth.

We stood with our mouths open and our eyes averted in shame. But Bernie wasn't looking for our approval. He didn't need our approval anymore. He only sought a signal that we had heard what he had said. He was simply sharing the good news.

With a squeal of delight, he left us standing there and ran to find another group. I can still hear his voice getting fainter as he made his way to the other end of the camp: "Good newth! Good newth! Jesuth lovth me!"

Regardless of how he might score on an intelligence test, Bernie understood on that morning what some men and women never grasp. Bernie knew that he had nothing to prove. Jesus loved him. He didn't have to produce, perform, or live up to the "norms" that surrounded him. Bernie didn't have to be popular. He had nothing to prove. He was free.

What liberated Bernie that day? The truth liberated him. Bernie wasn't healed of his affliction that morning, and I'm pretty sure he didn't go on to hold some lofty public office or to succeed in business. But I know he *did* go on without the desperation that had once shown in his face. He no longer frantically sought the approval of every passerby. The Spirit of God had revealed to Bernie the truth that had been there all along.

And all of the truth covered in the earlier chapters of this book—our ability to live the abundant life that God intended, the possibility of freedom from self-doubt and peer pressure, and our hope for positive self-esteem, for the discovery of purpose, for knowing the will of God, and for living a life with nothing to prove—all of it rests on a simple foundation of truth, the same truth God revealed to Bernie that day at camp.

Free to Live with Nothing to Prove

Oh, how the heavy chains of bondage cut into the shoulders of men and women who still try to prove their worth to the world! We were not created to beat our fellow humans in this race of life. We were created to run without the chains. We were created to be free to share our strength with those having less, to complement the diverse strengths of others, to discover God's purpose for our lives, and to live to our fullest potential. If we have proved anything with our lives, it is that we are incapable of living up to the glorious ideal that God had in mind. Read the following verse, one that we have too often used as simply an evangelism tool for converting "those sinners." It is much more than that; it is a beautiful reminder that we have nothing to prove:

> For all have sinned and fall short of the glory of God, and are justified freely by his grace through the redemption that came by Christ Jesus. (Romans 3:23–24)

Romans 6:23 reminds us that "the wages of sin is death"— not just the kind of death marked by a gravestone but also the living death marked by uninspired, hopeless lives. There is *nothing* you can do to prove your worth to God. Nor is there anything you *need* to do. Your worth was forever sealed, not by what you have done but by what *he* has done—by the price paid on the cross. The One who spoke creation into existence looked at you and me and saw that we were undeserving of his love. But rather than blindly administering a well-deserved death penalty, God extended his grace and sacrificed his Son so that we might live. In that moment, even the blades of grass shouted the same message as Bernie: "Good news! Good news! You've got nothing to prove!"

You can let the same truth free you to live with nothing to prove. If you long to get the most out of life, if you would like to know the secret of making each moment count for all it is worth, then resolve this minute to lay claim to the same truth that liberated Bernie. You are God's unique creation, put on this earth to do what no one else in history can duplicate. Do you believe that? God chose to pay the ultimate price so that you could live. He gave his innocent Son to redeem your soul so that you could experience, through forgiveness, some measure of God's original, glorious intent for your life. That puts your worth beyond measure. You need not waste another moment proving your worth to anyone. Instead you can maximize every second by living to the potential for which you were created.

Act on that truth!

Good news! God has taken care of it all. You are free to live. You have nothing to prove.

Part 2
LIVING WITH NOTHING TO HIDE

Chapter 6

IS MORALITY A FOUR-LETTER WORD?

*He who is enslaved to the compass
has the freedom of the seas.*

—Unknown

A Misguided Society

The first great principle to follow, if you are to get the most out of life, is to live with nothing to prove. The second is this: live with nothing to hide. It is impossible to operate at peak performance while wasting energy deceiving others—or deceiving yourself. Freedom comes only to those who have made a commitment to personal and spiritual integrity. And that commitment can be made only by those who have created in their lives a foundation for that commitment: a consistent and rational set of moral absolutes.

Modern society resists this idea with indignant fury, and there is a reason for that. Men and women who are trapped by living with something to prove yearn to be free. But first they must understand the true meaning of freedom. Today, people think of personal freedom as *a life unhindered by moral absolutes.* We live in a relativistic society in which the mere suggestion of moral absolutes brings howls of protest. Modern Western society has an unreasonable, emotional love affair with moral relativism, a love affair that defies common sense. The fact is that nowhere in creation can moral relativism be demonstrated as viable.

We live in a world governed by absolute laws. Those laws exist as evidence of the order inherent in all of creation. Followed, those laws bring freedom, allow us to solve problems, and lead to new and exciting discoveries. Broken, they result in chaos and death.

The most obvious and easily identifiable examples of absolute laws are those found in science. Scientists every day make new discoveries about the miraculous order in the universe. Not only do the discoveries they make reveal an absolute order operating in nature, the methods they use to make these discoveries are based on universally recognized rules of normal science.[1] Studies that don't follow the rules of the scientific community are not considered valid. There is no relativism in the laboratory.

The same principle is true of virtually every other domain of human activity. For example, adherence to the laws of medicine has resulted in freedom from diseases that once killed millions. Nightmare diseases like the black plague, leprosy, tuberculosis, and polio have been all but eradicated. The laws of mathematics and physics have opened new horizons of knowledge that were unthinkable just a decade ago. Your own ability to make sense of what is written on this page is based on *absolutes* concerning conventions of language and alphabet and your ability to reason. In fact, all ability to reason, to draw dependable conclusions from our thinking, is built on the same foundation. Without that foundation, you have no hope of knowing anything.

Dependence on *absolutes* affects every aspect of your life. Even those who decry and deny absolutes will, in fact, demand that certain absolutes be acknowledged and followed. If you were sitting in a 747 waiting for takeoff, and the flight attendant announced that the captain had never been to flight school, you would trample people to get off the plane. If you were lying on an operating table, the anesthesia just beginning to take effect, and the nurse informed you that the surgeon was a free-spirited woman who had never gone to medical school, then regardless of the amount of anesthesia in your blood, there would be surgical tubing flying everywhere as you jumped from the table. We demand *absolute* safety standards for our cars, *absolute* health requirements for our food, and *absolute* monetary regulations for our banks. We are emphatic about *absolute* rules for the sporting events we watch, even to the point of watching replays in slow motion so we can be sure the rules are *absolutely* followed.

We live in a world guided by the fundamental and absolute necessity of law. But that same world, in a startling departure from logic, refuses to accept the concept of universal *moral* law. The result has been emotional and social disaster. In his 1978 Harvard commencement address, Aleksandr Solzhenitsyn said, "[In the West,] destructive and irresponsible freedom has been granted boundless space. Society has turned out to have scarce defense against the abyss of human decadence."[2]

If we expect anything except moral anarchy, we must accept some universal definition of morality—an *absolute* definition, in other words—and strive toward that standard. Those who deny the existence of moral absolutes, of course, claim that defining morality in absolute terms infringes on personal freedom, destroys creativity, and demonstrates intolerance. But the truth is that gusto living, as we have defined it, must rest on an absolute moral system. Moral absolutes will not deny you the abundant life—far from it, they will enhance your ability to *achieve* it. If you seek to live to your full potential, then without moral absolutes, you will never achieve your goal.

The Cost of License

The broad and beautiful boundaries of God's love and guidance provide room for more freedom than we could express in a lifetime. Yet we spend more time questioning the placement of the boundaries than we do exploring the expanse of our freedom.[3] Our behavior reminds me of the cattle we raised on our Minnesota farm. They would forsake acres of lush green grass to stand with their necks stretched through barbed-wire fence, nibbling at the dusty, dry weeds growing by the road.

The basic nature of humanity has not changed since Adam and Eve. They were given a flawless paradise in which to live. God richly provided them with marvelous and abundant foods. Beautiful plants and animals decorated their unspoiled home. No discord marred their relationship, either with each other or with their Creator. They were free to go anywhere and do anything—freer than we can imagine. They were burdened with neither governmental regulations nor complicated laws. God made only one request: he asked that they not eat from one tree in the middle of the garden. Other than that, the world was theirs. Talk about freedom! Yet the forbidden tree quickly became the focus of their attention. Rather than enjoying their "heaven on earth," they stood as though mesmerized by the "dusty grass" on the other side of the only fence in the universe. Their fascination with the one forbidden tree, their blindness to the boundless glory around them, their refusal to accept God's one and only rule, opened the door to a lifetime of evil and pain—for them and for all their children. With one rash act, they destroyed their own freedom and made themselves slaves to the treadmill.

It's the same today. Refusal to acknowledge moral absolutes puts men and women in bondage to the very things they thought were expressions of their freedom. Sadly, an entire generation is shedding the last remnants of moral restriction as they flaunt their freedom from absolutes. They think they are free, because they refuse to acknowledge the natural boundaries that hold life (and society) together. But they are not free. Like Adam and Eve, they are naked, they are vulnerable, and they are lost.

A Loss of Meaning

Our society's rejection of moral discipline has cost us dearly. The sexual revolution, for example, has not led to the freedom it promised. It has led instead to fear, mistrust, and death. Our fascination with unfettered freedom at the expense of truth has eroded more than the moral fabric of society—it has undermined our understanding of history, literature, politics, and art. Modern art best exemplifies the decay that unlimited freedom has brought about in our culture.

I remember seeing, in the early 1960s, my first example of modern art. It looked like an explosion in a crayon factory. Paint and wax had been splattered at random on an empty canvas. I asked the artist what it meant.

"It means whatever you want it to mean," he declared.

"What do *you* think it means?" I pressed.

He looked at me as if I had just insulted his mother. "It means nothing," he sniffed as he turned to find some more enlightened people to talk with.

Someone paid a small fortune for that mess of nothing. But a few months later a monkey sat and randomly spattered paint on canvas—and the monkey's paintings sold for even more than that human artist's paintings had sold for. When I think of the mess our farm animals used to make—if only I had thought to lay a canvas down out in the barn, I could be wealthy today.

The breakdown of the art world has gone so far that today an "artist" can drop a crucifix in a glass of urine, take a picture, and call it art. Recently another "artist" received a grant that enabled him to paint the individual words of a poem on the sides of cattle. Once the crude letters were painted, the cattle were released to mingle with one another, "reconstructing" the poem randomly in the field. Who conceived of this "art" project? Who will purchase it? Where will they hang it?

When I was twelve, I painted a forbidden word on the side of one of our cows. No one paid me a penny. But *I* paid dearly for it when my father brought the cows in that evening.

My point is this: when you refuse to *define* something—when you refuse to acknowledge the boundaries that make it unique—in a very real sense, that form of expression ceases to exist. When the boundaries of beauty and craftsmanship in art are ignored, then everything is art—which means nothing is art. According to the art historian H. R. Rookmaaker, this is exactly what has happened to modern art.[4] Creativity and freedom, not to mention beauty and truth, are lost. Likewise, when you remove any absolute framework for establishing moral guidelines, morality ceases to exist. Indeed, Rookmaaker said:

> The crisis in the arts is an expression of a much greater crisis in our whole culture. That greater crisis is a spiritual one which affects all aspects of society including economics, technology and morality.[5]

It is our disregard for absolutes that has precipitated the crisis Rookmaaker is describing. When morality can no longer be defined, we relinquish our right to call *anything* moral or immoral. Those who selectively choose to ignore certain acts of immorality while trying to stand firm against the more abhorrent acts of immorality are on philosophical quicksand. We cannot be selective. Either there *are* moral absolutes or there are not. If there are not, then no moral judgment can be made about anything. Without the standards provided by a system of moral absolutes, murder and pedophilia are just as acceptable as adultery. Despite the obvious need for moral absolutes, they are usually dismissed in our society as an antique throwback to less-enlightened times. Unrestricted tolerance is the gospel of a new age, each of us doing what we think is right in our own heart. The result: moral and social chaos.

It's a Mad, Mad World

We live in an upside-down society that winks at sexual misbehavior but fights vehemently for the right to kill the baby conceived as a result of that behavior. We will spend millions to save a whale but refuse to spend a penny to bring an inner-city school up to minimum standards. As Barbara Schoener, the mother of two small children, was jogging near Sacramento, California, not long ago, she was attacked and killed by a mountain lion. A coalition of sportsmen raised nine thousand dollars to be donated to a trust fund for her children. The amount raised to care for the cub of the lion that killed her was twenty-two thousand dollars. Ken Watkins, president of the International Bowhunting Organization, said, "To give money to an animal that likely would have survived in the wild anyway and ignore the Schoener family's plight is heartless."[6] When moral guidelines are blurred, heartless actions result.

If doing away with moral absolutes is the sign of an enlightened society, then why is our society slipping into darkness? Mona Charen asks:

> And what have we wrought, in modern society, by jettisoning traditional standards of virtue? We have a decaying social fabric in which criminal behavior is rampant, family structure is fragmented, drug abuse, suicide and sexually transmitted disease are epidemic.

Look at the facts:

> From 1960 to 1990 ... the U.S. population has increased 41% and the gross domestic product has nearly tripled. At the same time, during those crucial 30 years, violent crime increased 560%, illegitimate births (the origin of so many pathologies) increased by more than 400%, the divorce rate quadrupled, the teen suicide rate increased by 200%, and SAT scores dropped by 80 points. ... We've fallen so far that we do not even agree on what virtue is. ... Ours is an age of moral confusion—for which we are paying a heavy price.[7]

There's an old catch phrase that's still used to fight com-monsense laws of moral value: "You can't legislate morality." The simple fact is this: all legislation is moral legislation. Franky Schaeffer put it this way: "All law is, in fact, some form of legis-lated morality. The question is whose morality will dominate."[8]

Clearly, our society demonstrates that rebellion and disre-gard for God's absolutes result in shallow substitutes for gusto living, substitutes that eventually lead to death. Freedom, on the other hand, comes from knowing and abiding by the truth found in the absolutes of God's Word. The Bible states it best: "Know the truth, and the truth will set you free" (John 8:32).

How, exactly, does the truth of an absolute morality set us free?

The Benefits of Limits

A Map That Shows Where the Holes Are

Jay Kesler, president of Taylor University, tells the story of a Boy Scout initiation ritual in which the boy to be initiated was led blindfolded through the forest to an old deserted cabin with a dirt floor. After everyone was assembled in the cabin, his friends told him that there was an old, dry well in the building— a *deep* old dry well. Then they told lies about careless children who had fallen to their death. To convince him further, the Scouts would place a small stone in the blindfolded boy's hand and tell him to carefully lean out and drop it into the well. When he dropped the stone, one of the boys would silently catch it. A couple of seconds later, another boy would drop a stone in the dirt at the far corner of the room. To the blindfolded boy, it sounded as if the stone had fallen into a deep well.

After disorienting the initiate by spinning him in circles, the boys would tell him that if he removed his blindfold, he would not be allowed to join their Scout troop. Of course, they would add, the same restriction would apply if he fell to his death down the well. Then they would leave the cabin and, through the open door and windows, watch from a distance.

Most of the boys subjected to this initiation never moved. Once they'd been left "alone" by the other boys, they were frozen in place the entire time they stayed in the cabin. They were paralyzed. Why? Because they were blinded and didn't know where the dangerous well was. For all they knew, a step taken in any direction could have been their last.

But there *was* no well—it was just an adolescent prank!

True. But in real life, the holes are numerous and deadly. Millions of people in our generation are blindly groping their way through life, with no direction, no sense of purpose or excitement—terrified that their next step will be their last, because they don't know where the holes are. Millions of others are wounded or dead because they ran wild, believing that there were no holes. They were wrong.

Why, when a disregard or denial of moral absolutes exacts such a high price, do so many continue to disregard them? Well, as stated earlier, the detractors of absolute morality claim that defining absolutes infringes on personal freedom, destroys creativity, and demonstrates intolerance.

Do the absolutes of God's Word infringe on personal freedom? In his landmark book *None of These Diseases,* S. I. McMillen, a medical doctor, amasses an incredible array of evidence that shows how many of God's laws literally protect us from killing ourselves. In the day of Moses, men and women were dying by the millions because they were following the unhealthy pseudo-medical practices of the Egyptians, which included the use of:

> lizards' blood, swine's teeth, putrid meat, stinking fat, moisture from pigs' ears, milk, goose grease, asses' hoofs, animal fats from various sources, excreta from animals, including human beings, donkeys, antelopes, dogs, cats, and even flies.[9]

These abhorrent practices, coupled with moral corruption, laid the groundwork for some of the most horrible diseases known in history.

However, when Moses led the great company of Israelites out of Egypt, the Lord gave him a most remarkable promise for the new nation:

> If you listen carefully to the voice of the LORD your God and do what is right in his eyes, if you pay attention to his commands and keep all his decrees, I will not bring on you any of the diseases I brought on the Egyptians, for I am the LORD, who heals you. (Exodus 15:26)

"The divine instructions were not only devoid of harmful practices but had many detailed positive recommendations."[10] Among those positive recommendations, God gave absolute instructions on how to quarantine infectious diseases, avoid harmful foods, and abstain from unhealthy sexual practices, and even gave detailed instructions on personal hygiene. Thousands of years later, "modern" medicine was still reluctant to recognize the validity of God's way. Countless millions of lives could have been saved down through the ages since God's law was given to Moses had people been willing to follow it.

No moral or practical absolute given in all of Scripture was ever designed to sap joy and adventure from life. God's absolutes had a positive, not a negative, purpose: providing the people he loved with guidelines to help them achieve the abundance he had originally intended for their lives.

The pilot who refuses to follow the rules of safe flight will die and take others with him. The surgeon who disregards the laws of medicine will destroy rather than heal. And the men and women who disregard the moral absolutes of life will fall far short of their full potential. Sin exacts its own deadly toll. We reap what we sow. Falling into the moral holes of life will rob you of your potential and may even lead to death.

A Springboard for Creativity

One of the arguments offered against moral absolutes is that they stifle creativity. All of life's experience demonstrates just the opposite. True freedom and true creativity spring from a foundation of absolutes. A disciplined life is, without question, superior in creativity to the aimless floundering of one who refuses to acknowledge moral boundaries.

In the domain of sports, for instance, it's the preciseness and skill of the Olympic athlete that brings tears to our eyes. Behind the dramatic flair of the ice-skater, and the freedom and grace of the gymnast, lies years of frustrating yet disciplined practice. The successful athlete is not the one who refuses to tune his or her body to its finest peak and who will not submit to the fundamentals of his or her sport. Would you buy a ticket and go occupy an uncomfortable seat in a stadium to watch lazy, uncoordinated, undisciplined men or women make a mockery of their sport? Not likely. Stadiums are filled with people who have come to admire those who are so disciplined in the basics that they are free to respond spontaneously to the unusual and demanding situations of competition.

The same is true of the master musician. The truly creative musician is one who so thoroughly understands and masters the basics that he or she is free to improvise and bring individual beauty to the art form. The foundation of his or her creative expression is absolute understanding of, and *submission to,* the fundamentals of music. No one shouts "Bravo!" during the orchestra warm-up. It is the mastery of a difficult score that moves us during a symphony performance. Discipline leads to excellence in every facet of life—and discipline requires a system of absolutes.

Absolutes—the Foundation for Living with Nothing to Hide

What's a chapter on moral absolutes doing in a book about living life to its fullest? What does all of this have to do with you?

Just this: acknowledging the legitimacy of God's moral absolutes and disciplining yourself to follow those guidelines is a prerequisite to gusto living. Moral integrity is *absolutely* essential to living with nothing to hide. If you lack a commitment to living by God's absolute standards, then you *do* have something to hide. You need not be confused about how to live with integrity if you accept the validity of God's standards.

"Delight yourself in the LORD, and he will give you the desires of your heart" (Psalm 37:4). People who know God's law and delight in it are not easily led astray. They know where the moral holes are and how to avoid them. And the heart's desires they pursue are the *true* desires of the heart, not the cheap substitutes that rob us of time, energy, and love, only to leave us empty. Those who delight in God's law have an inside track to gusto living.

Don't be misled by the popular philosophy that moral absolutes are outdated rules that will keep you from real living. Instead acknowledge God's moral absolutes and dedicate yourself to strive for the freedom they can give. Search his Word for the guidelines that can make gusto living a reality. Then, using the power he promises, fire up your life!

---

1. For information on the rules of normal science, see Thomas Kuhn, *The Structure of Scientific Revolutions,* 2d ed. (Chicago: Univ. of Chicago Press, 1970), chs. 2, 4.
2. Aleksandr I. Solzhenitsyn, *A World Split Apart,* trans. Irina Ilovayskaya Alberti (New York: Harper & Row, 1978), 21.
3. See Vernard Eller, *The Mad Morality* (Nashville: Abingdon, 1970), 7–9.
4. H. R. Rookmaaker, *Modern Art and the Death of a Culture* (Downers Grove, Ill.: InterVarsity Press, 1970), 161.
5. H. R. Rookmaaker, *Art Needs No Justification* (Downers Grove, Ill.: Inter-Varsity Press, 1978), 15. (First published by Inter-Varsity Press, Leicester, UK).
6. *WLPA Newsletter* (Summer 1994), 3.
7. Mona Charen, "Virtue Vanishing from National Character," *Rocky Mountain News* (April 1993), 53.
8. Franky Schaeffer, *A Time for Anger* (Wheaton, Ill.: Crossway, 1982), 25.

9. S. E. Massengill, *A Sketch of Medicine and Pharmacy* (Bristol, Tenn.: Massengill, 1943), 16, quoted in S. I. McMillen, *None of These Diseases* (Old Tappan, N.J.: Revell, 1963), 9.

10. S. I. McMillen, *None of These Diseases*, 10.

Chapter 7
THE PENALTY OF SIN

*Like a corrosive acid, unconfessed
sin burns a hole in the heart.*

I remember the first time I saw the pen. It was the most captivating, the most seductively attractive, thing I had ever seen. The bottom part of the pen was a beautiful emerald green, and the top was filled with clear liquid. Inside the liquid was an exquisite little baseball player with his glove opened upward, ready to catch a fly ball. Also encased in the liquid was a tiny baseball. By tipping the pen upside down, you could make the little ball slowly sink to the very top of the pen. If you were careful when you tipped it rightside up again, you could get the baseball player to catch the tiny ball.

I *wanted* that pen! The boy who owned it was generous. He let me play with it whenever I wanted. But I wanted more than that—I wanted to *possess* it. That desire haunted me every day, and one day when all the other students were playing outside, I sneaked into the classroom and stole the pen.

I remember how I trembled when class resumed. Life had suddenly become ugly. When the teacher called on me, I would jump. Was this it? Had I been discovered? I was sure my classmates knew—I could tell by the way they looked at me. Surprisingly, there was never any fuss about the pen being stolen;

perhaps the boy who owned it never reported it missing. But the secret plagued me.

In the days that followed, I hid the pen in several different places, never leaving it in one place for long before I would be seized by a fear that someone would find it there. I didn't want the pen anymore; my desire for it had been killed by the guilt and fear I felt. In fact, I was looking for an opportunity to return it. But I waited too long, because eventually I hid it somewhere so secure I forgot where it was, and I never saw it again.

Even today the memory of that school year is dominated by the memory of my secret. From the moment I slipped the pen into my pocket, its mystery and beauty were destroyed. (I never once got a chance to play with it after I stole it.) The fear and guilt that accompanied that theft became the central reality of my life for weeks. You may be thinking, *Grow up, Ken—it was just a pen!* I agree; my sin may seem pitifully insignificant in the glare of some of the evil that surrounds us today. But regardless of the size of my sin, its results were the same. In any degree or caliber, sin destroys. And hidden sin devastates. Living with something to hide is like trying to run a race with a millstone hanging around your neck.

Unfortunately, the stolen pen was not the only secret that plagued my life. I can also remember times as an adult when hidden sin strangled the joy and freedom from my life. There was a time when I was living one life at home, another life at church, and still another at the comedy clubs where I performed. I was constantly juggling my separate lives, hiding my inconsistencies. Eventually I began to wonder who I really was. Was I really the Christian my church believed I was? Or was I really the person my friends at the comedy clubs had come to know? Every time the telephone rang, I wondered whether somebody had found me out. Someone once said that the beauty of telling the truth is that you never have to remember what you have said. The beauty of living with nothing to hide is that you are free to be who God made you to be—no pretense, no deceit, no fear of discovery. What you see is what you get.

An Evil Motive

When I was finally freed from that charade of inconsistent, dishonest living, I began to openly share my experience with others. I discovered that many men and women are facing the same disabling problem. I am saddened by the number of my friends who have carried on hidden affairs until their marriages and families were destroyed or who have struggled alone with pornography until its addicting grip dominated their lives. Others held on to anger until it matured into hatred, casting a shadow of bitterness over everything in their lives. I've seen the pain of the secret alcoholic, of the person whose compulsive gambling is hidden from others, of the mom who secretly cultivates her prescription drug habit. The simple truth is, *sin kills*. It kills not just physically but emotionally and spiritually as well. The Bible says, "Be self-controlled and alert. Your enemy the devil prowls around like a roaring lion looking for someone to devour" (1 Peter 5:8).

Do you think I'm overstating my case? Listen as Charles Stanley discusses the following verse from the book of James:

> But each one is tempted when he is carried away and enticed by his own lust. Then when lust has conceived, it gives birth to sin; and when sin is accomplished, it brings forth death. Do not be deceived, my beloved brethren. (James 1:14–16)
>
> Sin is an agent of decay. Once sin is introduced into anything—a relationship, a community, or an individual—order and productivity begin to diminish. The term *decay* means "to pass gradually from a sound or perfect state to one of unsoundness and imperfection." Such is the nature of sin. Satan's goal was to undo what God had done. The introduction of sin or evil accomplished just that. Man's first sin was all it took to begin a chain reaction that sent shock waves throughout creation.[1]

There is a progression in sin. First, there's the seemingly innocent indiscretion. Then comes ensnarement. Finally death—certainly spiritual and emotional, and possibly physical as well—is knocking at the door. That progression doesn't come without our own complicity; it requires the nurturing of the sin. It requires secrecy. To whatever degree we practice sin and allow it to secretly grow in our lives, it takes control and eats away our God-given potential to enjoy it. Instead of living with gusto, we begin to rot. That which initially seems so innocent and harmless will eventually break forth with the full stench of decay— opportunity gone, love lost, confidence destroyed, joy forgotten.

Sin's destructive power can be conquered only by the cleansing power of God's forgiveness. That forgiveness, of course, is already there, freely offered as a gift. We need merely to accept it to enjoy its benefits.

If sin requires our own continued complicity to kill us, and if conquering it is as simple as confessing it and accepting God's forgiveness, then why is it so powerful in our lives? Because the most dangerous aspect of sin's attack is its subtlety. Satan doesn't come from the pit swinging a sword and screaming, *"Prepare to die!"* He comes smiling, offering pleasure, comfort, compromise. "Everybody's doing it," he whispers. "You want gusto living? I'll show you excitement beyond your wildest dreams." His arguments are persuasive. "The little secret you hide is nothing compared to the heinous crimes of others," he hisses. "As long as nobody gets hurt, what's the difference?" But Satan's motive never changes. He wants to destroy you. A fired-up life? He wants to put it completely out of your reach. He can't kill you just by *tempting* you to sin. But if he can get you to give in, to hide that sin and nurture it, then he's well on the way to putting you out of commission. Satan isn't interested in bringing you real joy, but he'll gladly fulfill your immediate desires in order to entice you to your death. Make no mistake—Satan's goal is to destroy you!

The Wages of Sin

Here are some of the ways that hidden sin eats away at your opportunity for maximum living:

Sin Alienates Us from God

First and foremost, sin separates us from God. Notice that I did not say it causes God to withdraw from us. (God *does* withdraw from sin—after all, he *hates* sin. See Psalm 5:5 and Romans 1:18. But God still seeks sinners, and in Christ he draws near to them, as explained in Romans 5:8 and 2 Peter 3:9.) His love is unconditional, and his forgiveness is always available. But Satan uses sin to place obstacles between us and God.

There has never been a time in my life when I was in disobedience to God and didn't feel that a barrier had been erected between us. God didn't lay one brick in that wall. I did it all. And I did it by believing the Deceiver. "He can't love you now, not after what you've done," Satan whispers to us. Filled with shame and self-loathing, we find it difficult to look into the loving face of God. So we hide.

After Adam and Eve sinned, how did they respond to the God who loved them? "Then the man and his wife heard the sound of the LORD God as he was walking in the garden in the cool of the day, and they hid from the LORD God among the trees of the garden" (Genesis 3:8). Adam and Eve hid from God, just as we do.

When you betray one who loves you, you find it uncomfortable to be in the presence of that person whose expressions of love only make you more uncomfortable. We try to think of ways that we have been treated unfairly in the relationship, so that our sinful natures can find an excuse for—and maybe even find some satisfaction in—our betrayal. "See," we reason, "you deserved it." But how do we stand before a holy God who has done nothing to deserve our betrayal—who has, in fact, made provision for the very sin that now drives us from him? Only God's Holy Spirit can enable us to stand before him.

So we must make a decision. Either we embrace the sin or we embrace the Savior. But it is impossible to embrace both. "No one can serve two masters. Either he will hate the one and love the other, or he will be devoted to the one and despise the other" (Matthew 6:24). If we choose to keep our sin a secret and embrace its seductive call, if we make a conscious choice to practice that sin rather than obey God, then we will turn away from the only source of our salvation. Our Bibles will lie unopened. Our places of prayer will be vacated. Christian fellowship will sour. Our Lord will be left standing with outstretched arms as we pursue the sweet, musky odor that is really the stench of death.

Sin Erodes Our Confidence in the Power of God

Sin also causes us to lose confidence in the power of God. Once we allow sin to get a grip on our lives, our instinctive response is to blame God for not delivering us from our bondage. *If he is so powerful, why can't I quit drinking? Why do I continue to demean those around me? Why do I give in to lust? Why do I lose my temper so easily?*

The simple truth is that God has not abandoned us. Jesus' death and resurrection have empowered us to say no to sin.

> No temptation has seized you except what is common to man. And God is faithful; he will not let you be tempted beyond what you can bear. But when you are tempted, he will also provide a way out so that you can stand up under it. (1 Corinthians 10:13)

As I look back at my own life, I can remember the very moment (sometimes two or three moments) when God offered me a "way out" from sin. Unfortunately, I can also remember the exact moments when I turned away from his offer of deliverance. That was true even with that pen I stole long ago. Before I put it in my pocket, there was just a second when God's quiet voice pleaded, "Put it back." Again, in the minutes before the students came back into the room, I had several opportunities to put it back—and then again, after they returned, the boy who owned it turned to me and asked, "Have you seen my pen?" How simple it would have been to say, "Yes, I was just playing with it. I have it right here." No questions would have been asked. But as God opened each door of escape, I turned away.

One of Satan's supreme desires is to drive a wedge between you and God. If he can't alienate you from God by shaming you into hiding, then he'll try to smuggle doubts about God's power into your mind.

Sin Destroys Self-Confidence

When we continue to sin and to hide that sin from God and the people we love, another danger presents itself: self-confidence dies.

At the very least, hidden sin causes us to lose self-control. As experimentation with sin becomes habit and habit becomes addiction, a sense of hopelessness takes over. Harry Shaumburg, author of *False Intimacy,* says that most men and women with sexual addictions have come to believe that they can't live without fulfilling their fantasies. Their lives are run by habit and desire gone wild.[2] The same can be said of almost any addiction and, to a lesser degree, other habits that control our lives.

God created each human with a will and a tremendous capacity for joy in using that will to make choices that lead to maximum living. Regardless of which sin entangles us, if we give in to it, if we hide it, we will weaken our ability to exercise that will. When that happens, we feel powerless and diminished, disgusted with our weakness; eventually we loathe ourselves. The resulting lack of confidence will affect our work, our relationships, and everything we touch.

At that point, depression knocks at the door, and creativity takes a nosedive. Everything is colored by our obsession with sating our desires and by the constant struggle to survive the consequences of sin. For many of us, every waking moment is overshadowed by that process.

I recently spent some time with friends who have smoked for years. Each day's schedule revolved around a few ounces of tobacco. As we traveled, stops had to be made so that they could smoke. Money was spent so that they could smoke. Medicine was consumed to combat the effects of smoking. Restaurants were bypassed because smoking wasn't allowed. Ask people who are in the process of quitting this habit how many times a day they think of cigarettes. They will tell you: constantly.

All that energy and time would make sense—if it were expended for a worthwhile cause. But to quench an uncontrollable desire to suck on a piece of paper filled with burning weeds—let alone weeds that drain the life out of you? I characterize smoking as a sin because of one thing: the destruction it causes to the body. I use smoking as an example here because of the nature of the habit. Smoking is not pleasant when you start; in fact, it's very unpleasant for most people. It requires a determined effort to continue, it's an expensive habit to maintain, and it has numerous unpleasant side-effects, not the least of which is the destruction of one's health.

I can think of a lot of other obvious sins that offer much more to the sinner in terms of immediate gratification. It's irrational to live a life so dominated by a meaningless weed. Yet millions of intelligent men and women allow *this* habit, smoking, to control their lives. I know: I was one of them. Regardless of how irrational a habit smoking is, to this day there are times when I am assaulted with a momentary desire to start it all over again.

Such is the power of sin. We can be tempted to yield to sin even when we know the dangers. A child will usually touch a hot stove only once. After that one bad experience, intelligence takes over, and hot stove tops are avoided. Yet we often suffer incredible pain because of our sins, only to return again and again to whatever burned us. That is the strategy of the one who seeks to destroy us, and it seems to be working. When we find ourselves caught in that self-destructive cycle, we may be powerless to stop it, but we're smart enough to see how stupid it is—and to loath ourselves for being so weak.

Jim walked out of a massage parlor in Los Angeles into the bright sunlight. It wasn't the first time he had visited one of the prostitutes who worked there, but it was to be the last. The powerful desire that had lured him to this place was gone for the moment, replaced by a sickening realization that he had once again betrayed himself and the people he loved. His self-disgust was overwhelming, and the Deceiver was quick to reinforce his feelings, convincing Jim that he was beyond redemption, without hope. A hundred times Jim had muttered, "Never again." But it was never very long before he was back. No one knew Jim's hidden sin except himself—and he could no longer bear the burden alone. This time, the shame was too much.

The note he left on the motel dresser was the only thing left behind by this once vital, potential-filled life. How the demons of hell must have leaned forward in anticipation as Jim wrote! And when he pulled the trigger, they undoubtedly jumped to their feet, cheering wildly as Satan threw back his head and laughed. This time he had destroyed not just his victim's self-confidence but his very life. It is Satan's ultimate victory.

Sin Hardens the Heart

One of the most sinister effects of hiding sin is the danger of becoming so hardened that we no longer hear God's warnings and calls to repentance.

I have always been amazed at a single verse found in the story of Jonah: "Jonah had gone below deck, where he lay down and fell into a deep sleep" (Jonah 1:5). What's so strange about that verse? Remember that Jonah had just received a verbal command from the Lord to go to Nineveh and preach against that city because of the rampant wickedness there. Rather than obeying God's command, Jonah ran to the city of Joppa and boarded a boat going in the opposite direction. That boat had barely gotten out of port when a violent storm threatened to tear the ship to pieces. Jonah was running from God! He was in the middle of a storm, his life in extreme danger, and he didn't even know it—he was sleeping!

When we first turn our backs on God to embrace some petty sin, our hearts pound and our minds race at the thought of betraying such a loving and powerful God. For days, guilt eats at our souls. But the next time our hearts don't beat so fast. After all, we already did this once, and no lightning came from heaven. No one in our families turned into a pillar of salt. The only consequence was an almost imperceptible change in our relationship with God. What kind of change? It's a little like the difficulty of making eye contact with someone whom you have wronged. It's an uneasiness of the conscience, an uneasiness that makes it more difficult to pray and to read God's Word.

Even so, Satan's persistent lie sticks with us. "That wasn't so bad," he whispers. "Once more can't hurt." So we do it again, reasoning that if we really get into trouble, God is loving and forgiving—he'll still be there.

Sure enough, this time it's easier—and the heavens are still devoid of lightning. After several times, we begin to wonder why we made such a fuss over such a little sin in the first place. Eventually the early-warning system is overridden. We find it easier and easier to continue in sin if we just ignore the alarms and shut out God's pleading voice.

That's a dangerous path. It leads to situations where family, job, mental health, reputation, and sometimes life itself are threatened. But by that time, we have grown so callous that we are numb to the warnings. Just like Jonah, we are asleep in the bottom of the boat while a life-threatening storm rages just outside.

Thank God for his mercy. Look at what he did to Jonah, the one who blatantly disobeyed him. God would have been perfectly justified in destroying Jonah. Yet after the fish deposited the rebellious prophet on the beach, "the word of the LORD came to Jonah a second time" (Jonah 3:1). What beautiful words! God gave him another chance.

But don't take God's mercy for granted. If you continue to wallow in secret sin, there is another danger, one that is worse than apathy and insensitivity to God's Spirit.

God May Let You Have Your Own Way

The most frightening words found in the Bible are these: "God gave them over." God said to the people of Israel, "My people would not listen to me; Israel would not submit to me. So I *gave them over* to their stubborn hearts to follow their own devices" (Psalm 81:11–12, emphasis added). Again, through Ezekiel, God said, "I also *gave them over* to statutes that were not good and laws they could not live by" (Ezekiel 20:25, emphasis added).

In case you're thinking that this is Old Testament stuff and doesn't apply to New Testament Christians, listen to Stephen's message in Acts 7:39, 42, and 51 (emphasis added): "Our fathers refused to obey him. . . . God turned away and *gave them over* to the worship of the heavenly bodies." Then Stephen added the words that would cost him his life: "*You are just like your fathers:* You always resist the Holy Spirit!"

The people were so angered with Stephen's message that they stoned him. Standing in the crowd that day was a man named Saul, one of the key figures in the persecution of Christians. But Saul was later to have an encounter with the living God. This man, an accessory to murder, would become an apostle who would die for the same cause that Stephen did. Saul not only came to recognize the truth in Stephen's words, he reemphasized them when he wrote a pleading warning to the Christians in Rome:

> For although they knew God, they neither glorified him as
> God nor gave thanks to him, but their thinking became futile

and their foolish hearts were darkened. Although they claimed to be wise, they became fools and exchanged the glory of the immortal God for images made to look like mortal man and birds and animals and reptiles. Therefore *God gave them over* in the sinful desires of their hearts to sexual impurity for the degrading of their bodies with one another. They exchanged the truth of God for a lie, and worshiped and served created things rather than the Creator. (Romans 1:21–25, emphasis added)

History reinforces the idea that the worst thing that can happen to humanity is to be left to its own devices—oblivious to the redeeming influence of a holy God. Without that influence, the sinful nature of the human heart quickly takes over. Before long, even reason is cast aside. We plug our ears to God's call. Carried to its limits, such a "God-vacuum" leads to the worst horrors of humanity. You can read in Ezekiel 20 how the people had begun sacrificing their own children and then celebrating the event with orgies. Serial killer Ted Bundy maintained that his passive and seemingly benign involvement with violent pornography led to the cancerous obsession that led him to murder and rape. James Dobson suggests that our present-day obsession with killing millions of innocent babies may be the result of the same kind of stubborn resistance to God. It makes one shudder to consider what will come next if we continue on this horrible path.

Regardless of what you think about pornography or abortion, the Word of God is clear about one thing: if we continue to hide our sin, if we embrace its lure rather than accept the forgiving love of God, then at some point, God will leave us to our own evil devices. From that point, it's just a short step to the discovery that our sin has grown into a hideous monster that we cannot control but that controls us instead—the same conclusion reached by Jim the day he walked out of the massage parlor in Los Angeles.

Live with Nothing to Hide

Throughout this chapter, I've used terms like "addiction" and "uncontrollable desires." Perhaps you've shrugged off what I've said, reasoning that those terms don't apply to anything you're experiencing. If so, you're in a position of great peril. You may not be addicted to any of the things I've mentioned. But to whatever degree you hide sin and allow it to grow in your life, no matter how socially respectable that sin might be, you will be missing the mark of the full potential that God intended for your life. That hidden sin also makes you vulnerable to the destruction that would bring so much glee to the Wicked One. Don't tell me I'm overstating the case. I've personally felt the heat of the Deceiver's lying breath and watched him get close enough (while I did nothing to stop him) to threaten everything that I hold dear. That's why I beg you: Please wake up. It's never too late to grasp God's rescuing hand.

"Yes," you respond, "God's forgiving hand is available to sinners. But I'm a Christian, and I've struggled with sin for years without experiencing victory. I know of God's sacrifice for my sin, and that's what makes my continued failure seem so evil. I'm beyond hope—I've already accepted Christ to no avail."

If that's what you're thinking, that's another lie from the same source that enticed you to the trouble you now face. Here's the truth: You are *still* a sinner saved by grace. God's grace is still available. Wake up and claim the forgiveness he offers. Only one thing can give you strength again and lead you to victory: his love.

There is good news for Christians: "The one who is in you is greater than the one who is in the world" (1 John 4:4). If you still wish to live life to its fullest and want to have power over the sin that so easily entangles—that power is still available. Not from your own determination. Not even from recognizing the tremendous cost that sin extracts from your life. But from the One who paid the penalty for that sin.

Today is the day to claim the power of God's Holy Spirit so that you may live the life of victory he desires for you. The choice is yours.

The next few chapters will show how to access the power to set yourself back on the track to realizing the full potential God intended for your life.

---

1. Charles Stanley, *Winning the War Within* (Nashville: Nelson, 1988), 26.
2. See Harry W. Schaumburg, *False Intimacy* (Colorado Springs: Navpress, 1992), ch. 1.

Chapter 8
WRITTEN IN CRAYON ON A PAPER HEART

Started out this morning in the usual way
Chasing thoughts inside my head of all I had to do today
Another time around the circle
Try to make it better than the last
I opened up the Bible and I read about me
Said I'd been a prisoner and God's grace had set me free
And somewhere between the pages it hit me like a lightning
    bolt
I saw a big frontier in front of me and I heard somebody say
Let's go!
Saddle up your horses we've got a trail to blaze
Through the wild blue yonder of God's amazing grace
Let's follow our leader into the glorious unknown
This is a life like no other
This is the Great Adventure!

—Steven Curtis Chapman

In chapter 6 of this book, we acknowledged the Word of God as the foundation of moral absolutes. We recognized the important role those absolute truths play in abundant living.

They guide us toward our life purpose identified in chapter 3 (remember?).

But not surprisingly, there is a problem. The problem is sin. Even though Christians are made righteous in Christ, our sinful nature ensures that we will fall short of God's ideal.

Martin Luther explained the paradox this way: "On this side of eternity, we are at the very same time completely righteous (in Christ) and completely sinful."[1]

Therefore we *will* fail. How we handle those failures can either cripple us or empower us for maximum living. We can allow guilt to drain the vitality from our lives, we can pretend to be perfect and deplete our energy by hiding the real truth from ourselves and others, or despite our weakness, we can recognize the remarkable grace of God that frees us to press toward the mark of his excellence. And therein lies the paradox: Our power to live according to God's Word will come not from raw effort expended to "be good" but rather from a humble awareness that he loves us in spite of our "lack of goodness." God is our sole source of strength, and his grace is so wonderful that he can create something good even from our mistakes (Romans 8:28).

Only those who live with nothing to hide have the capability of living up to their full potential. And living with nothing to hide is possible only when we begin to grasp the meaning of God's grace. Without that understanding, we will waste our lives by wallowing in guilt and deception.

But the Truth Hurts

Guilt kills. It drives people to use enormous amounts of energy in trying to hide the truth from themselves, from others, and even from God. There is only one antidote for the poison of guilt: unconditional forgiveness.

We Christians often use the term *grace*, but we seldom stop to consider what it means. Grace is defined as "undeserved favor bestowed upon sinners through Jesus Christ."[2] No wonder we seldom stop to consider its meaning. The very definition of grace requires that we recognize our sinful nature. To deny or hide the fact that we are sinners negates the concept of God's grace. Yet we waste millions of hours doing just that. Even though we are aware of the biblical truth that God demonstrated his love for us while we were sinners (Romans 5:8), we continue to offer up good deeds and busy schedules to prove that we deserve his love. That time and effort accomplishes nothing in terms of our relationship with God, but it does create a smoke screen that obscures from us the truth that we are helpless sinners, desperately in need of a Savior.

As a child, I had a way of dealing with problems like this. If one of my sisters was saying something I didn't want to hear, I would close my eyes, plant my fingers firmly in my ears, and hum as loudly as I could. No one could get through to me then; there was too much noise in my head. All of our effort to hide from our true nature by going to church, avoiding the Nine Nasties, or being an upstanding pillar of the community are like humming with our fingers in our ears. They don't change the truth of our desperate need; they merely drown it out. In fact, our effort to impress God and others with our "goodness" is really evidence of our disbelief. It's a denial of Christ's finished work on the cross. Perhaps that's why God described our pitiful attempts at righteousness as filthy rags: "All of us have become like one who is unclean, and all our righteous acts are like filthy rags; we all shrivel up like a leaf, and like the wind our sins sweep us away" (Isaiah 64:6).

We struggle endlessly against an undeniable, simple, painful truth: we are sinners in need, and God loves us just as we are. There is *nothing* we can do to earn his love. That may be painful to accept, but that is exactly what makes his grace so wonderful—it's free! And claiming its power frees us from the grip of sin—frees us to maximize our lives.

The Benefits of Grace

Grace Frees Us from Doubt

I have met many sincere Christians who doubt that Christianity works. They offer as evidence their own inability to live righteously. All their lives, they have tried to prove that they are good Christians. And all their lives, they have failed to live up to their own expectations, let alone God's.

Satan loves to manipulate this misconception to paralyze believers. He points to our temper, our selfishness, our impure motives and thoughts, our struggle with alcohol, or our conflict with a spouse or child. Then he mocks us: "If Christ is so powerful, why do you continue to struggle with sin?"

The answer is simple: *We are sinners.* Why should this come as a shock? It's old news—over two thousand years old. Our sinfulness is the reason that God sacrificed his Son. We *say* we believe this—but when, instead of accepting his forgiveness, we try to prove that we deserve it, we call our own belief of the gospel into question. We respond to Satan's mockery by determining to do better next time.

Have you ever prayed this prayer: "Lord, I'll never do that again"? That's a prayer that is often prayed more than once—about the same thing we said we would never do again. The truth is that we are prone to doing *that thing,* whatever it is, over and over until the day we die. Is there no hope for us, then? God forbid. The power of Christ, and the power of Christ alone, can give us victory over sin. But that victory will only be realized when we admit that our own efforts at righteousness are in vain and that we are powerless without him. Jesus said, "I am the vine; you are the branches. If a man remains in me and I in him, he will bear much fruit; apart from me you can do nothing" (John 15:5).

Rather than focusing on ourselves, either on our own self-effort or on our sin, we need to forget ourselves and focus on Christ and on his righteousness. Christ is the source of our freedom from sin. The apostle Paul understood this truth when he wrote, "I can do everything through him who gives me strength" (Philippians 4:13). When we waste our time by trying to pull ourselves up by our bootstraps, we do not act as if we understand this truth. And all we end up with is broken bootstraps.

Society avoids confronting the sinful nature of man because of the belief that this idea diminishes human worth. If there were no God, or if God were not a loving and forgiving God, then society's assessment would be correct. But there *is* a forgiving God! Our unworthiness only magnifies the value that his sacrifice placed upon our lives. Our value stems not from what we have done but from what *he* has done—*despite* what we have done. The person who avoids confronting and acknowledging his or her sinful nature will find it difficult to truly experience God's forgiveness. To whatever degree we believe we are deserving of God's grace, to that same degree we diminish his grace.

Grace Frees Us to Love

Good works are not like bringing to God some offering that will make him love us. There are no works good enough to accomplish that. So what role do good works play? They're an important part of the abundant life, all right—the Bible is clear about that. But it's a matter of getting things into the right perspective. The truth is that proper motivation releases powerful performance, and not vice versa. If we think of our achievements as proof of our worth to God and to others, we will quickly be persuaded into thinking that our good works make us good. This perspective leads to guilt and disappointment. But as Martin Luther taught, "[The Christian] does the works out of spontaneous love in obedience to God."[3]

Envisioning our achievements as flowing out of an all-consuming love for God clears the way to operate at full potential. As Luther said:

> Behold, from faith thus flow forth love and joy in the
> Lord, and from love a joyful, willing, free mind that serves

one's neighbor willingly and takes no account of gratitude or ingratitude, of praise or blame, of gain or loss.[4]

When we are properly motivated, we are released to accomplish more. We are also less vulnerable to the doubt and guilt that strangle so many. But what *is* this motivation, and how does one get it? There is only one motivation that will take you to the ultimate freedom that God intended for your life: a passionate love for God. But how *does* a person love God? Do you wait for a feeling to overwhelm you? Do you do good things?

Trying to love God by being good leads to disappointment and frustration. The problem is that we *fail* at being good, and those failures soon convince us that we're incapable of loving him. We end up either spinning our wheels in hectic activity that goes nowhere or giving up and turning our backs on the only One who can lead us to the abundant life we so deeply desire.

Several years ago my wife, Diane, and I met with a counselor. At the time, I was devastated by the inconsistencies in my own life, feeling utterly helpless to become a better husband and father—a better child of God. The gap between the man I wanted to be and the man I was seemed impossible to jump. I had lost all hope in the struggle for spiritual and personal growth. I felt like Paul did when he said, "I know that nothing good lives in me, that is, in my sinful nature. For I have the desire to do what is good, but I cannot carry it out" (Romans 7:18). Paul had also once said that he was the chief of sinners (1 Timothy 1:15). Compared to him, I felt like the commander in chief.

During that counseling session, I asked how I could more effectively demonstrate the love of Christ in my relationship with my wife.

"It's your desire to love and obey God," the counselor replied, "that provides the motivation to keep you on track in your marriage."

I wilted. My spiritual life was already in disarray. Many times I had little desire to love and obey God, or at least little faith that I *could* love and obey him. Even when I did feel that desire, it was often short-circuited by temptations or circumstances that caused me to react as if I were still a slave to sin. Finally, out of frustration, I asked the counselor, "How does one maintain that desire? I *want* to love God more, but I don't know how. Does obedience make me love him more? Does reading the Bible make me love him more? How about getting more involved in church? Praying more? Doing more good things?" The truth was that I had already tried all of those things and did not sense a deepening love for God. In fact, I was getting tired of trying to do good. I was developing a deep conviction that my weakness was evidence that I didn't love God, and that there was no way to change that. And if I didn't love God, then perhaps he was also finding it difficult to love me.

Like most counselors, my friend did not give me a direct answer. (I hate that.) I continued to struggle with the question for several weeks. A deep depression settled over me. I wondered whether I could face another day. That was the only time in my life that the thought of suicide entered my mind as a possibility.

Deep down I knew the truth: obeying God does not make us love him. Instead loving God is what leads us to obey him. That obedience, in turn, results in peak performance. And peak performance is what the abundant life is all about.

But knowing all that didn't help, because I was still missing the first part of the equation. What *produces* love for God?

The answer to that question came written in crayon. At the darkest and most dangerous moment of my struggle, I paused to straighten my desk. God used that moment to intervene. While cleaning out a drawer that had accumulated junk for years, I found a heart cut out of red construction paper. I recognized it as my own creation, probably a remnant of my early Sunday school years. The scrawling letters, written in crayon, formed these words: "We love him because he first loved us. 1 John 4:19."

Obviously, I had learned this truth as a child. Why, then, had I spent most of my life living as though the message had read "We love God by proving that we are worthy of his love"? Good works (and the abundant life) *flow out* of love for God. Love for God does not flow out of good works. How does one love God? The answer is, We love God by never forgetting that he first loved us, and that he loved us in spite of our sin.

We can relax—the secret is out! We are sinners who have nothing to offer to God to make him love us. We have nothing to hide and nothing to prove. We have nothing to hide because the sad nature of our sin is already known—there's no point in trying to hide a secret that isn't a secret. And we have nothing to prove because we *can't* prove our worth. Our worth is found solely in Christ.

A word of caution: without the healing power of his unconditional forgiveness, true insight into the evil condition of your heart can be hazardous to your health. It can lead to depression and despair that seem beyond hope. Satan waits for this vulnerable moment. He would like nothing better than for you to see the depth of your own depravity but not see the cleansing power of the blood of Christ. That's when he'll try to convince you to give up—or even, like our friend Jim in the previous chapter, to end it all. It was only because the Holy Spirit of God led me, in the midst of my own dark moment of the soul, to the drawer with the crayon message "We love him because he first loved us" that I was able to escape that depression and despair. That message filled the room with light and hope, and it lit in my soul a fire to serve him as I had never served him before. The years AC (After Crayon) have been closer to abundant living than anything I had experienced before that day.

I have nothing to hide! God loved me when I was at my worst. Experiencing God's love and forgiveness has freed me from my bondage to sin and especially to guilt. Now I am free to be what he created me to be. God's message to me was the same message he gave to Paul: "My grace is sufficient for you, for my power is made perfect in weakness." So I am able to share in Paul's conclusion: "Therefore I will boast all the more gladly about my weaknesses, so that Christ's power may rest on me" (2 Corinthians 12:9).

Sometimes, seeing our own depravity and lack of acceptability—our true self—isn't easy, especially for those of us who've grown up in the church. It may be easier for people who have come to Christ from a background of destructive living. They have already peered into the pit of hell; they know what they have been saved from and therefore are more capable of recognizing the grace of God in their lives than those who have lived a "respectable life" from birth. Many who grew up in nice Christian homes, who attended Sunday school and Bible camp, who occupied a pew every time the church doors opened, who didn't "smoke, drink, or chew, or date girls who do," have a difficult time seeing their own sinfulness. The truth still remains: "The heart is deceitful above all things and beyond cure. Who can understand it?" (Jeremiah 17:9).

Too often we view ourselves as relatively acceptable in God's sight. We want to believe that he loved us because of a good streak he saw in us. On the other hand, we can't understand how God could love or forgive the "really bad" people. Does God really love serial killers? Does he love the child molester we read about in the paper? Does he love Manuel Noriega? When one of these people claims to have found new life in Christ, we are filled with doubt and even revulsion. We want to believe that there are people who are beyond God's redemption. But not us, of course—we fall well within the scope of God's love and forgiveness. We are, after all, more deserving of God's love than those people.

But is the proud pastor of a large, well-respected church any less of a sinner than the drug dealer? The Bible is clear: Because of our sins, we have *all* fallen short of deserving God's glory.

This is not to say that all sinful behaviors are equal in their consequences. Murder or rape are definitely worse than telling a white lie or failing to put a quarter in a parking meter. But both categories of sin are symptoms of a spiritual problem deep within the persons who commit them. *All* sin, whether great or small, separates us from a righteous and holy God.

Luis Palau hit on the following insights in an article he wrote for *Christianity Today:*

> Honest evangelicals will admit to . . . disbelief when they hear that a Dodd [a serial child-killer] or a Noriega—or twenty years ago a Colson—turned to Jesus and found forgiveness. Though we claim that "everyone who calls on the name of the Lord will be saved" (Romans 10:13), we act as though the gospel is for really nice people.
>
> If it seems strange that grace can rescue child killers and drug traffickers, we have not begun to fathom God's ocean of mercy. Nor have we peered long enough into our own hearts, for even as I write this, I am searching for explanations to the grievous moral failures of several Christian friends. The answer comes only when I truly believe that God can save a wretch like me, not just a nice guy with a few problems.[5]

I remember when as a child, I visited the bowery of a large city. There, in the midst of those alcohol- and sweat-saturated laborers, I first heard someone say, "There but for the grace of God go I." I have used that saying on several occasions in my life. But now that I have been forced to face the wickedness of my own heart, I have stopped saying it. That statement, it seems to me, implies that the grace of God does not extend to the person in the gutter. The speaker seems to be saying, "But for the grace of God I might be as wicked a sinner as he is." The truth is, I *am* as wicked a sinner as he is.

If the grace of God is not extended to the very worst of sinners, it can't be extended to you and me. What criteria make us more worthy? Not our goodness in relation to the wickedness of those around us. If that were true, we would constantly be living with something to prove, and whenever we failed, we would live with something to hide.

Where I grew up in Minnesota, we struggled constantly with dandelions. About midsummer they would begin to bloom, blemishing the most luxurious green lawns with blotches of yellow. With relish I would start the lawnmower and systematically destroy the whole yellow lot of them in our yard. Because the obvious evidence was gone, I was deceived into thinking that the problem was gone. But within a week, the dandelions would be back, thicker than ever. Why? Because nothing had been done about the *roots*.

Sin works much the same way. We mentally construct categories that allow us to grade our sin on levels of badness. The bigger the dandelion bloom in our lives—in other words, the more evident and obvious the consequences of the sin—the worse the sin. Rarely do we see our own sin as being in one of the worst categories. But that approach is deceiving. All sin springs from the same root, and it's that root that God is concerned about. The root of sin—unbelief and rebellion against God—can sprout either a serial killer or a pious, prideful bulwark of the community. Most of us would categorize the latter as better than the former. Isn't the prideful bulwark of the community more deserving of God's love? Yet both spring forth from the same root, and the sins of one, as much as the other, necessitated the death of Christ on the cross.

The Bible emphasizes acknowledging and confessing our sin and unworthiness. That is not a condemnation of humankind—it is instead a confirmation of God's unconditional love. God doesn't want us moping around declaring, "I'm a worm." His desire is to see us operating at peak performance, with nothing to prove and nothing to hide, praising him for his marvelous love.

> Very rarely will anyone die for a righteous man, though for a good man someone might possibly dare to die. But God demonstrates his own love for us in this: While we were still sinners, Christ died for us. Since we have now been justified by his blood, how much more shall we be saved from God's wrath through him! For if, when we were God's enemies, we

were reconciled to him through the death of his Son, how much more, having been reconciled, shall we be saved through his life! (Romans 5:7–10)

That is gorgeous truth. The response to such love is more than just Christian *behavior*—it is Christian *character.* The resulting behavioral changes come not from trying to be a better Christian but rather out of a broken and genuinely grateful heart. Literally and simply, *we love him because he first loved us.*

I once commented to the pastor of one of the largest churches in America that I appreciated his ethical integrity over such a long period of leadership. "Don't compliment me," he said. "It should be expected of everyone."

Perhaps. But his answer left me strangely disturbed. Shouldn't we fall on our face and thank God for his grace any time we exhibit qualities of righteousness? Integrity, love, gentleness, kindness, meekness—these are not natural qualities of the human race. Wherever they are found, they are reflections of a loving God. Given our sinful nature, a more reasonable expectation for our lives would be for us to languish in jail because of some heinous crime.

When we see someone lying in the gutter, we are seeing ourselves. It's just a different kind of dandelion showing. The same root causes our particular sin. Instead of pointing out that we aren't as bad off as that poor derelict, perhaps we should thank God that his grace is available for both of us. The saying should be: "There I go—thank God for his grace." Perhaps if we said that, we'd feel more desire to see the destitute person experience that grace as well.

The result of recognizing our own inability to live up to God's ideal is an incredible awareness of the depth of his love. Our response can only be loving obedience—not to gain his approval or to prove our lovability but simply to love him. Our works become the by-product of recognizing his love. A sense of mercy to those around us is another by-product of seeing our true sinfulness.

The root of all sin is disbelief in the love of God. Eve didn't believe that his loving provision was enough. She yielded to the Devil's lie that she needed more. She believed that by eating from the tree, she would gain something the Creator couldn't give her. We are just as deceived when we believe that his sacrifice on the cross was not enough and that we must do good to please him and gain his love. Only when we recognize his incredible love and accept his unconditional forgiveness for ourselves are we free to live with nothing to hide. Our imperfect sinfulness can then be openly confessed in anticipation of his overwhelming forgiveness. The experience of that forgiveness, along with the total encompassing power of his love, then drives us to want to obey and serve. We become servants—but willing and gleeful servants, responding in love to the Savior who responded in love to us. Then, perhaps for the first time, we can live with nothing to hide.

---

1. See Martin Luther, *Commentary on the Epistle to the Romans,* Romans 4:1–7.
2. *The Zondervan Pictorial Bible Dictionary*, Merrill C. Tenney, ed. (Grand Rapids: Zondervan, 1967), 322.
3. *Martin Luther's Basic Theological Writings,* ed. Timothy F. Lull (Minneapolis: Augsburg Fortress, 1989), 611.
4. Ibid.
5. Luis Palau, "Notorious Conversions," *Christianity Today* (March 1993), 20.

Chapter 9

A FOUNDATION FOR CHANGE

Therefore, there is now no
condemnation for those who are in
Christ Jesus, because through
Christ Jesus the law of the Spirit of
life set me free from the law of sin
and death.

—Romans 8:1–2

Understanding and accepting God's grace opens the door to a freedom that cannot be achieved in any other way. It allows us to build our lives on the most solid foundation possible; it frees us from the bondage of the law and changes the focus of our lives from *obeying rules* to *loving God*. In the process, God gives us the power to obey.

Our personal efforts are not sufficient to enable us to obey the law that brings discipline and freedom. Rather it is Christ's grace that motivates us to love and obey. Although abiding by God's laws—his guidelines and principles for behavior—is essential to gusto living, those who try to do so under their own power will be in for a big disappointment. Love is the *only* motivation that will keep us on the moral track to freedom. This doesn't mean that we should put forth no effort, merely trusting God to keep us pure. It *does* mean that personal effort is not the starting place.

Our ability to understand this process and to consistently apply it to our lives depends partly on a correct understanding of the purpose of God's law. Why did he establish his law in the first place?

There are three reasons. First, God did not give us the law as a means of salvation. When he gave the law, he already knew that we couldn't live up to it. Paul said to the Romans, "There is no one righteous, not even one" (Romans 3:10). Later in the book of Romans, he reemphasized this point, saying, "There is no difference [between Jews who felt they had kept the law, and Gentiles who had no regard for the law], for all have sinned and fall short of the glory of God" (Romans 3:22–23).

Second, the law was not given as a ten-step program for achieving God's full blessing. Paul is emphatic about this point: "You who are trying to be justified by law have been alienated from Christ; you have fallen away from grace" (Galatians 5:4).

Third, the law was not given as a yardstick by which to measure human goodness. Again, Paul says, "Therefore no one will be declared righteous in [God's] sight by observing the law" (Romans 3:20).

So if no one could live up to God's perfect ideal, if no one was able to keep the law, then why was it given? The law was given to demonstrate how helpless and lost we are without Christ. It testifies to our inability to even come close to living up to God's glorious ideal for our lives. John Stott put it in a nutshell: "Nothing can convince us of our sinfulness like the lofty, righteous law of God."[1]

Like a microscope, the law magnifies the true depth of our sinful nature. "Therefore no one will be declared righteous in his sight by observing the law; rather, through the law we become conscious of sin" (Romans 3:20).

However, there is a beautiful flip side to that coin. In exposing our sinful nature, the law also magnifies the grace of God and drives us to seek him. Paul explains:

The law was added so that the trespass might increase. But where sin increased, grace increased all the more, so that, just as sin reigned in death, so also grace might reign through righteousness to bring eternal life through Jesus Christ our Lord. (Romans 5:20–21)

Whenever we attempt to keep the law to prove our own righteousness, the result will be disappointment, bondage, and impotence. Only the forgiveness offered by Christ can release in us the power of the Holy Spirit and so enable us to live holy lives. When we fully accept that forgiveness and focus on our relationship to the One who delivered us from the law, we are motivated to obey him.

Deciding to obey him, however, still leaves us with the question, *How* do I develop the discipline to set and keep moral guidelines for my life? The answer is not to try harder but rather to trust him more. The shift from one focus (self-effort) to the other (God's grace) may in some ways seem subtle, but that shift means the difference between a growing maturity and a dead, hopeless legalism.

If our focus is on loving God and accepting his grace rather than on rigidly trying to keep the law, then why not live it up and sin all we want? After all, God's grace will always be available. The Roman Christians wrestled with that question almost two thousand years ago. Paul was quick to point out the erroneous assumption behind that question. It is our very concentration on God's grace that *triggers* our desire to keep the law. After explaining in detail how God's grace, through the sacrifice of Christ, is the only thing that makes us righteous before God, Paul says to the Romans, "For we maintain that a man is justified by faith apart from observing the law. . . . Do we, then, nullify the law by this faith? Not at all! Rather, we uphold the law" (Romans 3:28, 31).

Paul emphasizes again and again that focusing on the grace of God does not lead to uninhibited sin. Just the reverse is true. God's grace leads to commitment that brings holy living. It is that holy living that puts us in line with God's intention for our lives and on track for gusto living.

> What shall we say, then? Shall we go on sinning so that grace may increase? By no means! We died to sin; how can we live in it any longer?...
>
> Do not offer the parts of your body to sin, as instruments of wickedness, but rather offer yourselves to God, as those who have been brought from death to life; and offer the parts of your body to him as instruments of righteousness. For sin shall not be your master, *because* you are not under law, but under grace. (Romans 6:1–2, 13–14, emphasis added)

We do not keep the law to obtain God's grace. *Because* of God's grace, we keep the law.

Philip Yancey addressed this question in an article in *Christianity Today*. "If we approach God with a 'What can I get away with?' attitude, it proves we do not grasp what God has in mind for us." Those who genuinely experience God's forgiveness will have a very different reaction, Yancey explains. "If we grasped the wonder of God's love, the devious questions that prompted Romans 6–7 would never even occur to us. We would spend our days trying to fathom, not exploit, God's grace."[2]

Suppose I tell you that if you will love me with all your heart, you can do anything you want to me—and suppose that you *do* love me with all your heart. What will you choose to do? Your love will compel you to do only those things that bring me joy. Likewise, it will be our love for God that gives us the strength and discipline to live with victory over sin.

In this chapter, we'll examine five steps necessary in establishing the moral discipline to follow God's guidelines and move ahead to maximum living:

1. Start from the right foundation.
2. Determine the standards you will live by.
3. Stand together with other believers for support.

4. Understand that overcoming sin is a long and painful process often characterized by repeated failures.

5. Always remember the true source of your power.

Building Character from the Inside Out

When our focus is simply on obeying rules, the moral boundaries of our lives are established by outside forces—those that set the rules and those that monitor our compliance. Even when the moral guidelines we are following are God's guidelines, they are not God himself—in other words, we are controlled by someone or something other than the God who lives within us. When we are in that position, changes in the outside forces that keep the guidelines in place can have profound effects on our ability and motivation to keep the guidelines.

Here's an example: One of the most troubled periods of my life came when I left the ministry of Youth for Christ and went into secular work. My life took a moral nosedive. Only after recovery did I begin to understand what had happened. The truth was, I had never established the right base from which to live a moral life. While in the ministry, I had developed a moral lifestyle that was motivated by outside pressure rather than by a relationship with the One who loves me. My moral behavior and good judgment did not spring from a sense of joy in my salvation and in my freedom to return God's love. Instead I lived in response to those around me, in an effort to meet their expectations. It just so happened that for the first half of my life, those around me were Christian people who rewarded my good behavior with praise and acceptance—and punished bad behavior with rebuke and disfavor. My church, my family, and my peers at Youth for Christ—not God, and not me in response to God—set the boundaries for my behavior. This was through no fault of the Christians around me; it was me who was in the wrong.

Because my life was guided by the responses of the people around me, my behavior changed when I changed the people around me. When I entered the entertainment world, my new group of friends did not have the same moral expectations that my Christian coworkers at Youth for Christ had had. I was no longer rewarded for "Christian" behavior. Now I was rewarded for being a part of the crowd. From a motivational aspect, this was not such a big change. I was still allowing the crowd to set the standards for my life. It was just a different crowd.

It was a rude awakening to discover that my faith was much weaker than I had thought. My life was not driven by purpose; it was not controlled by inner goals. It was controlled by the outside pressure of whatever group I was trying to impress at the time.

God never intended for *any* group of people to be the moral foundation of our lives, whether it be church friends or secular friends. Only inside-out motivation is strong enough to stand in the face of temptation and failure. And that comes only from a growing love relationship with the God that lives within us.

In the movie *A Stranger Among Us,* Melanie Griffith plays the part of a woman who falls in love with a devout Jew who is preparing for rabbinical ministry. It is obvious that he has also grown to love her. In one scene, he responds to her seductive advances:

"I can't."

She counters, "You mean you won't?"

Confused, he asks, "Is there a difference?"

There's a *big* difference. Every year, thousands of teenagers leave home and head for college to start their journey as adults. Within months, many of these young people leave the "faith of their fathers" behind. This is sad but not surprising. The reason their lives change so drastically is that they relied solely on the "faith of their fathers" or on the faith of their church. That faith had never really become their *own.* It was merely a shell of real faith, developed by outside influence. When faced with temptation during their high school years, they probably responded, "I can't—because my parents won't allow it." Or perhaps they responded, "I can't—it's against my religion." That kind of motivation works only when the parents or church still have a direct influence on a young person's life. That's why those first college years are often times of such dramatic and sometimes traumatic change. For the first time, these teens are removed from all of the people who have influenced their lives. Only the convictions that are *personal*—that come from the inside out, that are *their* convictions rather than their *parents'* convictions or their *church's* convictions—will stand. These personal convictions are not "I can't" convictions; they are "I won't" convictions.

The man who doesn't plan to watch X-rated movies in his hotel room because it is against his religion will someday realize that his religion is not affected by, nor his church notified of, the choices he makes in the privacy of that room. That man will, on that day, be very vulnerable to the seduction of those movies. Similarly, many have given in to the temptation of adultery even though it is forbidden by their religion. They resolve that moral dilemma by simply leaving their church and dropping whatever pretense of faith had kept them from adultery before. Presto! Once the outside pressure is gone, the standards can easily be tossed aside.

The person who, over time and regardless of his surroundings or his company, continues to focus on Christ and his love is the one who operates from a solid foundation. The secret of that person's victory is the power of the Holy Spirit and the positive motivation that springs from experiencing Christ's love. When temptation arises, his answer is, "I don't *want* to—and I won't." He "doesn't want to" because no matter how powerful the temptation, the desire to respond to the love of Christ is greater. Only standards that have been built from this "inner" base of love will be powerful enough to keep us on track. Inside-out motivation cannot easily be affected by outside pressure.

God gave us the law so that we would recognize our own sinful condition. From that vulnerable position, we are able to see and appreciate the unfathomable grace he demonstrated for us. Once we have recognized the fully unconditional nature of God's love, we find ourselves motivated to obey him with a deep, inwardly anchored motivation stronger than any other. Even when we fail, this love drives us to pick ourselves up, acknowledge God's forgiveness, and continue to obey him. That obedience results in the physical and spiritual blessings that accompany moral discipline. Building on the foundation of love will not guarantee a perfect life, but it will bring us closer to his intended will for us—maximum living—than if we built our character on any other foundation.

So the first step in establishing the moral discipline that will lead you closer to gusto living is to *start from the right foundation*—and that foundation is to recognize and accept the limitless love that Christ demonstrated for you. Honestly survey your life and pinpoint those behavioral principles that are there only because of outside influence. If they are incompatible with Christ, get rid of them. But if they fit well with the godly life, allow the Spirit of God to make them yours from the inside out. Do this and you will find that as you continue to grow in grace and respond to God's love, you will be able to stand strong in the face of temptation.

Know Where You Stand
Before You Have to Stand There

The second step that will help you establish moral discipline in your life is to *determine the standards you will live by before you face real-life situations*. One of the most dangerous attitudes you can adopt is, "I'll cross that bridge when I come to it." Unless you want to be overwhelmed by the seductive power of sin, you need to decide how you will cross the bridge long before you stand at the precipice.

Know what you stand for before you have to take a stand. That is the principle that made champions of Daniel and his three young friends when they were all held captive in a strange and pagan land. They were faced with the twin temptations— power and wealth. In addition, they were threatened with death if they didn't follow Babylonian practices that were in direct contradiction to God's revealed will.

But these four men had set standards for their lives, and they had determined—*before* they were captured—that they would defile neither their bodies nor their God. Had they waited to "cross that bridge when they came to it," in all likelihood they would have faded into history as insignificant remnants of a captive culture who allowed their faith to be swallowed up by a brutal conquering nation. But they were prepared for their moment of destiny by their commitment: "But Daniel resolved not to defile himself with the royal food and wine, and he asked the chief official for permission not to defile himself this way" (Daniel 1:8).

Decisions of principle must be made before the heat of battle. Daniel predetermined that he would not defile his body by eating forbidden food. Because of that strength of character, he and his friends went on to remarkable achievement. Part of their success was due to the fact that they did not meet these challenges unprepared. They had established principles like those we discussed in chapter 3 as a foundation for their response to life. They didn't take a "wait and see" attitude. And look at the results. Under threat of death, they still refused to eat the unhealthy food that the king had offered. But God rewarded their faithfulness, and they were blessed with clear complexions, healthy bodies, and wisdom beyond any of their peers.

Later when Nebuchadnezzar ordered Shadrach, Meshach, and Abednego to worship the golden image of himself, their resolution was as solid as a rock. Again they faced death for disobeying a direct order of the king. And again their response rang with confidence:

> Shadrach, Meshach and Abednego replied to the king, "O Nebuchadnezzar, we do not need to defend ourselves before you

in this matter. If we are thrown into the blazing furnace, the God we serve is able to save us from it, and he will rescue us from your hand, O king. But even if he does not, we want you to know, O king, that *we will not serve your gods or worship the image of gold* you have set up." (Daniel 3:16–18, emphasis added)

The three needed no meeting to determine how they would respond. Long before this challenge, they had decided what their reaction would be.

Later when Daniel was threatened with death unless he stopped praying, he never flinched. This was another of his standards that was immovable. Daniel's daily prayer was not a whim or option—it was an unshakable part of his life, born of his appreciation and respect for God.

Now when Daniel learned that the decree [outlawing prayer] had been published, he went home to his upstairs room where the windows opened toward Jerusalem. Three times a day he got down on his knees and prayed, giving thanks to his God, *just as he had done before.* (Daniel 6:10, emphasis added)

Daniel's ethical commitment could not be compromised. There was a reason the administrators of Nebuchadnezzar's kingdom had tricked the king into passing a law that outlawed prayer: it was the only way they could get Daniel. They had investigated his life with the tenacity of a *Washington Post* reporter and could find nothing wrong. To get Daniel, they had to make illegal something that was actually good, because Daniel had nothing to hide:

At this, the administrators and the satraps tried to find grounds for charges against Daniel in his conduct of government affairs, but they were unable to do so. They could find no corruption in him, because he was trustworthy and neither corrupt nor negligent. Finally these men said, "We will never find any basis for charges against this man Daniel unless it has something to do with the law of his God." (Daniel 6:4–5)

What a testimony! If the government unleashed all of its power in order to find some fault in our lives, would the results be the same? I can tell you this: I hope *my* life is never subjected to that kind of scrutiny. In Daniel's life, they couldn't find so much as an unpaid parking ticket. What do you suppose gave Daniel the power to live such an exemplary life? I can't help but believe that his faithfulness was due in large part to his commitment to live every moment for God. His life was not a random, reactive response to changing life-situations. It was a proactive effort directed at being everything God wanted him to be. As a result, God delivered him from the claws of lions and from the grasp of evil men and put unprecedented power in his hands.

One of the reasons my wife, Diane, and I were able to celebrate our twenty-fifth wedding anniversary was an oath. Standing at that altar years ago, we predetermined that only death would part us. In times of stress—when we faced the difficulties that destroy many marriages—that oath made the option of bailing out unthinkable. Today many weddings don't even include the oath "till death do us part." There is no predetermination to make it work—and as a result, it *doesn't* work. Couples enter marriage with the idea that they will cross the bridge of trouble when they come to it. The smallest conflict, the least discomfort, the first temptation—and the marriage is up for grabs. Timothy George describes the power of commitment in marriage:

> There comes a time in every lasting marriage when the roses have faded, the music has stopped, and the candlelight flickers. Looking at one another across a plate helper, you know the only thing that keeps you going is the fact that once upon a time, in the presence of almighty God, you said to one another, "I do."[3]

Recently I watched as the astronauts completed a successful mission to fix the Hubbell space telescope—a task requiring

technology and precision far beyond the scope of my imagination. One wrong move, and the entire mission (costing many
millions of dollars) would be in jeopardy. But their success on
the mission had been prepared for by hundreds of hours of
tedious rehearsal. Over and over, for weeks before they left for
space, they had simulated every task to be performed, going over
procedures for any imaginable contingency. When the time
came for the real thing, they knew just how to respond.

No less attention should be given to our journey of faith. If
we are to live with nothing to hide, if we are to have any measure
of victory in the face of Satan's unrelenting attack, if we are to
even come close to Daniel's example of integrity, then we must
have in place the biblical principles by which we will live—and
we must predetermine our response for each situation. Cross
each bridge *before* you come to it, and you will find the crossing
easier when you actually arrive at the bridge.

One of the most powerful examples of this kind of commitment is demonstrated in the life of a modern-day Daniel. In an
age when the press is scrutinizing the integrity of preachers of
the gospel, looking for the smallest grain of dirt they can show
the world, they haven't had to look far. It seems that every time
they turn over a stone, they find greed, hypocrisy, and blatant
immorality, all of which deserve their disrespect. One man, however, has lived a life that has earned him the respect of even the
press: Billy Graham. I first became aware of his integrity when
he came to Denver for a crusade. I watched as the press worked
to dig up something "newsworthy" about his life. But they found
no dirt. In the midst of a stench of disclosures concerning television evangelists, Dr. Graham's life was a breath of fresh air.
Finally it was his unique integrity that found its way to the front
pages of the Denver papers. *That* became the story.

How does a man who has enjoyed such influence and power
remain strong in the midst of the temptations that come his
way? What is his secret? Why have we not read about the moral
downfall of Billy Graham? Maybe it's because as a young man, he

sensed the hand of God on his life (just as, in fact, God's hand is on the life of every one of us) and made a commitment to live a holy life. That's the difference. Long before there was such a thing as the Evangelical Council for Financial Accountability, Billy Graham and his team members made a commitment to avoid fiscal temptation by opening their books to the public. From the very beginning it was decided that Billy Graham would receive a modest salary and that he would live in relative simplicity. Long before sexual scandals rocked the foundation of "Christian" television, Billy Graham and his team made a pact among themselves that each would not allow himself to be alone in a room, or even in a car, with any woman other than his own wife. They didn't wait for situations of vulnerability to occur and then see what would happen; they rehearsed a battle plan against what they knew would be one of Satan's attacks. They didn't wait for the Devil to back them into a corner before they decided what to do. They identified the Devil's corners and established plans so that they would never find themselves there.

Billy Graham enjoys the respect of the secular press not because he is the most profound preacher ever to live. His reputation and influence have stayed intact not because he has established a great public-relations department. By the power of the Holy Spirit, he determined in his heart not to defile his body or the gospel of Christ. He planned his response to Satan's attacks before they happened, and he gathered a group of like-minded men who were willing to hold each other accountable to those commitments. Perhaps that is why even in today's secularized society, he is one of the most respected men alive. He and his band of coworkers have lived with nothing to hide.

Don't Go It Alone

Neither Billy Graham nor Daniel tried to go it alone. Daniel and his friends made themselves accountable to one another, as did Dr. Graham and his colaborers.

From the very beginning of time, God intended for people to work together in order for them to be at their very best. In the Garden, he created a partner for Adam. Jesus sent his disciples on their missions in twos; he also encouraged believers to stand together and draw from each other's strengths. Throughout the Scriptures, God refers to his people as a body—a body able to function at its peak when all the parts are working together. The man or woman who sets out alone to live a holy and exemplary life is likely to be doomed to failure. This, then, is the third step in establishing moral discipline in your life: *surround yourself with like-minded men and women, in a relationship of mutual accountability.*

In *The Defense Never Rests*, a videotape, Os Guinness uses the analogy of the football huddle to explain the importance of this concept. In the huddle, team members develop a plan of action. Every member knows his role and responsibility before the play begins. After the play, the team huddles again to hold one another accountable for their performance, to regroup, and to develop another plan of action.[4]

As you determine the principles by which you choose to live, "huddle" with trusted friends and ask for their help. One of the reasons that Alcoholics Anonymous works is because of the help that alcoholic men and women give each other. When tempted to "fall off the wagon," they call and tell a trusted friend about their struggle. Many find a strength in this accountability, a strength that had eluded them when they tried to go it alone.

At its best, this kind of teamwork goes a step further. Not only should we have friends who are available when we need help but they should be vigilant (and willing) enough to tell us where and when we need help even *before* we call. Rehearse with each other your weak points that may draw Satan's attack, and decide together what your response will be. I have a group of men who call me to find out whether I'm struggling with temptation. They don't wait for me to call them, and when they call, their questions are blunt and to the point. They are not afraid to tell me if

they think I am sliding toward danger. I don't enjoy this process.
It's easy to feel hurt or to rebel at their "intrusion" into my life.
But I need it. Our struggle with temptation is a life-and-death
battle. Satan doesn't wish only to take the gusto from our lives—
he lusts for our complete destruction. "Be self-controlled and
alert. Your enemy the devil prowls around like a roaring lion
looking for someone to devour" (1 Peter 5:8).

Without the objective intervention of caring friends, it's too
easy to rationalize wrong behavior or to isolate ourselves for the
very purpose of sinning in secret. Without the help of friends, it's
too easy to fall into Satan's traps—and not even know we're
there. Christian friends can see our lives from a different perspective. This is one of the roles that God intended for the
church to play. Unfortunately, we can be members of a church
for years and still not develop the kind of relationships that allow
for such intimacy. It is not pleasant to have someone point out
areas of your life that need growth. It is even more painful to listen to someone identify blatant sin in your life. It isn't necessarily the church's fault that we do not have these relationships;
often, it's by our own design. In his book *Inside Out,* Larry Crabb
explains:

> We devise strategies designed to keep us warmly involved
> with each other at a safe distance. We live to gain life from
> each other and to protect ourselves from whatever we think
> is life-threatening.[5]

You won't find that establishing and maintaining these relationships is easy. It takes a great deal of time, energy, and
courage. But it's *necessary* for survival in the world in which we
live. Because "the heart is deceitful above all things, and desperately wicked" (Jeremiah 17:9 KJV), it is almost impossible to
be totally honest with ourselves. Lewis Smedes explains:

> What makes self-deception so hard to overcome is that
> we never consciously set out to deceive ourselves. A liar may
> get up in the morning and say, "I'm going to lie to my wife

today." But nobody ever says, "I think I will lie to myself
today." This is the double treachery of self-deception: first we
deceive ourselves, and then we convince ourselves that we are
not deceiving ourselves.[6]

Others can better see the smoke screens we put up to avoid
confronting our own sin. Those closest to us are often aware of
weaknesses we can't see. I remember taking, in college, a test
that required me to write down how I perceived myself. My classmates also had to write down their perceptions of me. When we
compared those descriptions, it was clear that those closest to
me were aware of aspects of my life to which I was blind.

If we are to live with nothing to hide, we must allow trusted
friends to expose those parts of our lives that are hidden to us.
From the loving perspective of our Christian brothers and sisters, we can gain the strength necessary to stand firm in the
midst of temptation.

Hope for the Loser

Despite our best efforts, despite our sincere motivation to
love God because he first loved us, we will sometimes fail miserably. And sometimes, after repeated promises, we will fail again
and again and again. This chronic failure often leads to discouragement and despair. It can even lead people to turn their backs
on the Christ who is their only hope.

The fourth step in establishing moral discipline in your life
is to *realize that overcoming sin is a long and painful process
that is often characterized by repeated failures.*

We need to understand three things about sin. First, we
must realize that "perfection" will never be realized on earth.
John wrote, "If we claim to be without sin, we deceive ourselves
and the truth is not in us" (1 John 1:8).

Second, we must also remember that God forgives our sin.
"If we confess our sins, he is faithful and just and will forgive us
our sins and purify us from all unrighteousness" (1 John 1:9).

Third, we must recognize that overcoming habitual sin is a process. Many times, it can be a long process. Years of habitual sin may take years to conquer. Lewis Smedes writes about our addiction to sin:

> The best wisdom suggests that many of us go through three phases on our way into and out of addiction.
>
> First phase: We freely do something that gives us pleasure. Since it gives us instant pleasure, we choose to do it again. And again. And again.
>
> Second phase: We lose our power to say no to the desire. We are caught—maybe very quickly, maybe after years. Either way, however, we are out of control.
>
> Third phase: We admit to ourselves that we have lost control and that we cannot get it back again on our own. We face up to the fact that we are shackled. And when we've suffered too much, we seek help in our helplessness.
>
> The trip back to control is a long and painful journey, too long and too painful for some to finish. But the people who get there are usually the ones who surrender to the truth that they had lost their way.[7]

It is a "long and painful journey," but we have been promised that God will provide the resources and stamina to make the journey a success (see 1 Corinthians 10:13). Of course, we will stumble from time to time, but that is no reason to abort the journey. A child learning to walk will experience many falls. But she struggles back to her knees, then to her feet—and is soon on her way again. The process of moving from helpless infant to walking child takes time. It's a process. The same is true for maturing in the Christian walk.

Many Christians have struggled with habitual sin for years but with perseverance have finally found victory. In the article "I Found Freedom," Colin Cook explains how he overcame years of bondage to homosexual sin. First he had to grasp two truths: that he was helpless and that he had been freed from the power of sin by Christ's death and resurrection. Cook notes:

A switch seemed to flip on in my mind from a negative to a positive mind-set. Never since my conversion had I so greatly sensed the magnificence of Jesus.…

[The] reality that would take years to unfold through experience was telescoped into weeks of time. The prison door was open. No matter how long it took, I knew that I could ultimately walk free.[8]

Cook's transformation from guilt-ridden Christian bound in sin to one who could stand "blissfully, gratefully free" was neither quick nor easy. Through much perseverance and prayer, and with the steadfast support of his wife, he slowly experienced more and more freedom from the grip of sin. Cook declares, "Despite my stumbling, God did not let go of me." [9]

What do we do when we fail miserably? We must confess our sin, look to Christ, get help from friends, and patiently continue on our journey, trusting that God will not let go of us.

Remember the True Source of Power

"How-to" helps for living a life of victory over sin are well and good. If, however, they do not grow out of the proper motivation—loving God because he first loved us—and if they are not grounded in the true source of power, eventually they will all fail. The best summary of the nature of this battle and our preparation for it comes from the Word of God. In his letter to the Ephesian Christians, Paul said, "Finally, be strong in the Lord and in his mighty power" (Ephesians 6:10).

Notice where the power comes from. It is not in our discipline; it is not in how hard we try. That verse in Ephesians doesn't say keep a stiff upper lip, keep on trying, never give up, or just reach down and pull yourself up by your bootstraps. It says to be strong in *the Lord* and in *his mighty power*. Only *his* love, *his* grace, and *his* power will help us prevail. That is the fifth step: *remember the true source of our power, and realize that we are impotent without it.*

Paul goes on in that chapter to talk about the armor that will protect us from the Devil. But even this armor is, for the most part, a defense supplied by God to keep us from being annihilated in a battle beyond our understanding—a battle that, without God's power, we are unable to win.

We will not move any closer to the full and meaningful life we ache for until we learn to live with nothing to hide. Let Christ into the secret corners of your life. Allow him to identify those things that must change, and be ready to use every weapon at your disposal to be free from Satan's influence as you make those changes. A prayer from Psalms and a promise from Romans identify the attitude that will make the difference and the promise that will keep us trusting God:

Search me, O God, and know my heart today,
Try me, O Savior,
Know my thoughts I pray.
See if there be some wicked way in me.
Cleanse me from every sin
And set me free.
("Cleanse Me" by J. Edwin Orr, adapted from Psalm
    139:23–24)

Everyone has heard about your obedience, so I am full of joy over you; but I want you to be wise about what is good, and innocent about what is evil. The God of peace will soon crush Satan under your feet. The grace of our Lord Jesus be with you. (Romans 16:19–20)

---

1. John R. W. Stott, *Basic Christianity* (Downers Grove, Ill.: InterVarsity Press, 1980), 70. (First published by Inter-Varsity Press, Leicester, UK).
2. Philip Yancey, "Why Be Good?" *Christianity Today* (March 1994), 28–29.
3. Timothy George, "Cause I Was Called, You Fool!" *Christianity Today* (December 1993), 15.
4. *The Defense Never Rests* is available through the Coalition for Christian Action in Pittsburgh, Penn .

5. Larry Crabb, *Inside Out* (Colorado Springs: Navpress, 1988), 55.
6. Lewis B. Smedes, *A Pretty Good Person* (San Francisco: Harper & Row, 1990), 74.
7. Ibid.
8. Colin Cook, "I Found Freedom," *Christianity Today* (August 1989), 23–24.
9. Ibid., 24.

Chapter 10

NOTHING TO HIDE

The man was innocent.

Despite the legions that had been sent from hell to attack him, despite the demonic voices whispering discouragement, abandonment, and vengeance in his ears and promising deliverance—for a price—he never gave in to the monstrous temptations that could have destroyed his mission. His purpose had been decided before the worlds were formed, and he did not waver from that path.

Now he lay on the ground, spitting dirt and blood, trying to breathe. His legs had crumpled beneath him. The beatings, the physical exertion, and the emotional anguish of the past few days had taken their toll.

The small, boisterous crowd that had been following had suddenly grown quiet when he fell. Slowly they surrounded him, wondering what his next move would be. He heard the chink of chain-mail armor and the hiss of a sword being drawn; he sensed the jostling crowd moving back. A sneering soldier yanked him to his feet, nearly pulling his arm out of its weary socket. Two other soldiers lifted the crude cross that had forced him to the ground and placed it on the shoulders of a man who had not moved back far enough.

Even without the weight of the cross, the man stumbled as they shoved him up the hill. By the time they reached the place where he would die, blood and sweat mixed with tears of anguish streaked his holy face. When they drove the nails into his hands, the hardened soldiers never winced—but several who had followed had to turn away.

Those who knew him and heard his muffled cries of pain felt their own hearts tear. It was happening so quickly. This one in whom so many had placed their hope was now caught in a vortex of injustice that could not be stopped.

Suddenly the heartrending cries of his mother pierced the darkening, ominous air. It was going to happen; nothing could stop it.

Even his followers, as they watched, knew that no savior would appear and rescue him at the last moment. That was what made this moment so unbelievably horrible: this was the Savior. If he could not save himself, who else could possibly save him?

As the cross dropped jarringly into its rock-lined hole, Christ's eyes closed in pain. A mocker dashed forward to spit on the base of the cross. In contempt he began to shout a blasphemous epitaph.

Then the Savior's eyes opened. They looked directly into the eyes of his mocker. The epitaph caught in the man's throat. In the eyes of the man on the cross, he saw no hatred, no revenge, no pitiful pleading. He saw only love. He wanted to run, but he could not. He was still standing there, frozen in place, when Jesus shouted, "Father, forgive them, for they know not what they do!"

He was there still when Jesus cried out and died. But he was no longer standing in defiance. He lay face down on the ground, weeping. How could anyone love him so?

The sacrifice of Christ plays through my mind time and again in many different ways. I wonder: *What was it like from his mother's perspective? From the perspective of those who followed him? What was it like for the soldiers, or for those who followed just out of curiosity? Did they have any hint of the glory that was unfolding? Did they sense the purity of the One they crucified?*

Sometimes I wonder: *What caused his death? Certainly the physical pain and trauma contributed. But is that what killed him?*

Psychologists and physicians tell us that one of the most destructive forces in life is guilt. People hide from the knowledge of their own wrongdoing and persist in painful denial that can result in sickness and even death. One of the primary reasons that men and women shy away from and never experience the beauty of trusting relationships is that they are hiding their true selves, deathly afraid of the very intimacy they crave, because they fear painful rejection. People hide secret infestations of sin because they are unaware of the forgiveness available to them.

This unresolved guilt takes a terrible toll. Doctors say that each year thousands develop diseases that would never have invaded their bodies except for the stress that accompanies guilt. Guilt's weight can open the doors to depression that is so deep it's like staring into a black hole in space. The psychic and spiritual pain of unresolved guilt far exceeds most physical pain. Thousands take their own lives every year because they don't feel capable of bearing the pain of guilt; they feel as if they've been brought to the brink of hell itself.

All of us have experienced that hell-on-earth to some degree. In the face of that memory, consider this. On the cross, Jesus took upon himself the guilt (and the anguish and pain that accompanies it) for every sin you and I have committed—plus all the sins committed by all the men and women who have ever lived or ever *will* live. If Jesus truly took the guilt of the world upon himself, then how could he, in his frail human body, possibly have survived? Even without the physical suffering of the cross, he might have died just from bearing that load. An autopsy report could have read: *Died of a broken heart induced by the pain and emotional trauma of unbearable, undeserved guilt.*

And what was Christ's motive for enduring this? He did it so that we would not have to. He knew that the ultimate penalty for sin was death. He died so that we would not have to suffer that guilt and pay that ultimate price.

Guilt is the by-product of hiding unconfessed sin. Until we allow Christ to wash us clean and free us from guilt, the abundant life is only a whispered pipe dream. But those who, through faith, trust in what Christ did on that cross for the forgiveness of their sin can experience the lifting of that guilt. A blinding burst of light vaporizes their darkness and gives them the power to live with nothing to hide.

The anguish and terror of the cross was necessary because of our sin—sin that could not be dealt with any other way. As ugly as that day appeared to the stunned, uncomprehending observers, it hid an unfolding beauty of hope and redemption. As Jesus hung on the cross so that guilt and death would not destroy our souls, every fiber of his flesh and every drop of his blood cried out: *Good news! You have nothing to hide!*

Part 3

LIVING WITH NOTHING
TO LOSE

Chapter 11

Nothing Ventured, Nothing Gained

The fear of death does not keep us from dying, it only keeps us from living.

—Paul C. Roud

A policeman arrived at the scene of an accident before the dust had even settled. He found that a wealthy young man had been thrown clear just before his Mercedes plunged over a steep cliff and crashed onto the rocks, far below, in a ball of flame. He was standing along the roadside at the top of cliff, weeping—and bleeding profusely from the stump at his shoulder, all that was left of his arm.

"My Mercedes! My Mercedes!" the young man howled.

"You ought to be thankful you're alive," the amazed policeman said.

"But it had twenty thousand dollars' worth of options," the man whimpered, staring down at the burning wreckage at the bottom of the cliff.

"There are things more important than that stupid car," the policeman insisted, guiding the injured man away from the cliff.

"We've got to get you to a hospital. Your arm has been torn off—you could bleed to death!"

The young man looked down and noticed for the first time that his arm was missing. Horrified, he screamed, "My Rolex! My Rolex!"

An exaggeration? Perhaps—but not by much. Today's headlines are full of stories of people who destroy their lives out of fear of losing their material possessions. They murder to collect insurance policies, defraud to gain the financial leverage to build business empires, and steal to accumulate what they cannot keep. They are willing to risk their life to gain *things*—but fear prevents them from risking their *things* in order to gain life, the greatest and most rewarding risk of all.

Fear—it is one of Satan's most lethal weapons, and he uses it to keep us from living with nothing to lose. He brandishes this weapon in three main areas of our lives: fear of failure, fear of pain, and fear of death. Because we fear failure, we live with something to prove—filling our lives with possessions and accomplishments in an attempt to validate our personal worth. The fear of pain tempts us to live with something to hide, seeking easy solutions rather than the more painful but effective process of dealing honestly and thoroughly with our sin, our broken relationships, and our need to change.

Always lying just below the surface of our consciousness is the fear of death. We *know* it's there, but we refuse to look it in the eye. Keep busy, keep smiling, keep achieving—just don't acknowledge the inevitable. As a result, we die before we die, living as if we'll live forever and failing to cherish the moment today. We miss the opportunities to enrich our relationships with those whom we love. And most of all, we sell our chance at abundant life for cheap substitutes of the real thing. Paul C. Roud is right: The fear of death doesn't keep us from dying—it only keeps us from living.

The cumulative effect of fear on our lives is devastating. If there is one thing that true faith should demonstrate, it is the banishment of fear from our lives. People who live with nothing to lose do not allow fear to rule them. They are willing to trust God, willing to risk, ready to endure the pain that accompanies emotional and spiritual growth. Understandably, many of us avoid risk and pain—they are, after all, unpleasant. But it is a mistake to assume that living for Christ results in a life free from risk and pain. Indeed, God often uses risk and pain to bring us to maturity, as 1 Peter 1:6–7 explains:

> In this you greatly rejoice, though now for a little while you may have had to suffer grief in all kinds of trials. These have come so that your faith—of greater worth than gold, which perishes even though refined by fire—may be proved genuine and may result in praise, glory and honor when Jesus Christ is revealed.

The book of James echoes this truth:

> Consider it pure joy, my brothers, whenever you face trials of many kinds, because you know that the testing of your faith develops perseverance. Perseverance must finish its work so that you may be mature and complete, not lacking anything. (James 1:2–4)

But if you listen to the way Christians talk, you might get the impression that risk and pain are not positive things in the Christian life. Most of the testimonies given in today's churches follow a predictable line:

"I was in pain—but I prayed, and the pain disappeared!"

"We were running out of money, and I still didn't have a job. We were afraid we were going to have to sell the house. And then God came through, and I got a job that pays more than the one I had before!"

I'm not saying that God shouldn't or doesn't answer our prayers about our needs, or that he scoffs at material blessing. But the tone of our prayers and testimonies, in some ways, only verifies the true source of our security and faith: our personal comfort, our jobs, and our health. Too often we sound as if we can't afford to lose the symbols of our success and as if God is simply the insurance policy that keeps us from that loss when other means fail. By adopting that attitude, we express disdain for the concept of suffering for Christ.

In reality we are asking God to give us back our security blankets. Modern Christians are afraid to take risks. In some Christian circles, it's even considered an ungodly thing to do. We believe that the Christian who has lost a job or is struggling with a rebellious child must have done something wrong—after all, "real" Christians don't suffer!

Tell the apostles that. Look at the lives of those who followed Christ. To the fishermen he said, "Drop your nets [translation: quit your job] and follow me." To the adulterous woman he said, "Go and sin no more." To each of us he pleaded, "Take up your cross and follow me." Most of our Christian heroes, the ones whose lives inspire us, paid a price to follow God's instruction. They experienced less physical comfort, less financial security, and less acceptance by their peers because of their choice. Yet if we could interview them today, do you imagine that they would say, "I wish I'd followed Christ less and enjoyed a little more physical comfort and affluence"?

Where *is* this spirit of trust and faith today? If Christ himself knocked at your door tomorrow and said, "Drop everything and follow me. I will show you adventure and gusto living beyond your wildest imagination," what would your reaction be? I know the first frantic thoughts that would run through my head: *But I've worked years to get to where I am. What about my house? How will I support my family? What will the neighbors think?*

And yet "Drop everything and follow me" is *exactly* what he said to the disciples—and they *did*. It was no small thing for the fishermen to drop their nets. Fishing was their only source of income. But they did it—and in the process, they were beaten, they sometimes went hungry, and eventually their allegiance to the Savior cost some of them their lives.

Were there days when the disciples wondered whether they

had made the right decision? There must have been. But in the end, I doubt that any of them wished they could have just stayed fishermen. If that had been their attitude, they would have thrown in their sandals long before they were forced to pay for their faithfulness with their lives.

God isn't going to require each of us to sell all that we own and follow him to a martyr's death. But he does require that we be *willing* to give up everything and that we follow him until we die. Unfortunately, we often refuse even his smallest requests as we cling to some insignificant trinket that offers nothing.

Today if we are persecuted for our faith or if following Christ results in a smaller income or a less-prestigious position, we are tempted to ask God what we have done wrong. We give lip service to a Savior who died for our sins—then we live for the savior of material wealth and social comfort, knowing full well that the savior of wealth and comfort is no savior at all. Jim Elliot said, "He is no fool who gives what he cannot keep to gain what he cannot lose." Inspiring words—but let's stop and think for a moment before we applaud his faith. If he was right, there are more fools in Christendom than we would care to admit. If he was right, I must count myself among them. I too have missed much of the gusto that God intended for my life, and I did it by trying to gain things I will not be able to keep, at the expense of the eternal wealth that God has promised.

The bodybuilder's motto is theologically correct: "No pain, no gain." Larry Crabb touched this nerve with his best-seller *Inside Out,* in which he identified a simple truth: spiritual and interpersonal maturity is impossible without pain. The inward look required to hone a life dedicated to the Savior—in our relationship with him as well as in our other relationships—can be excruciatingly painful. The confrontation and intimacy of a good marriage hurts. It is impossible to be a good parent without experiencing the pain that comes with unconditional love. Rather than trusting Christ to sustain us through the pain toward better relationships, we ask him to take that pain away—or we look for material and social diversions to anesthetize us.[1]

But even more than our intense effort to avoid pain, even more than our frantic attempt to achieve material success in order to insulate ourselves from suffering, there is one final idol, one that we hang on to at all costs: life. We hang on to life as though we don't believe in eternal life. We clutch this life as though we believe we can keep it. Jesus said, "Anyone who does not take his cross and follow me is not worthy of me. Whoever finds his life will lose it, and whoever loses his life for my sake will find it" (Matthew 10:38–39).

The fear of death destroys abundant life. Those who die to this life *gain* life—not just eternal life but the true essence of what God meant our life on this earth to be. The Bible says that death has lost its sting. The Bible says that Christ rose from the dead so that we could be raised up with him in newness of life.

Someone once said that we should live each day as if Christ had been born yesterday, had died and been raised from the dead today, and is coming again tomorrow. From God's timeless, eternal perspective, that is exactly what happened. We sing about it, we worship because of that truth, we testify to it—but we so often live as if we don't believe a word of it.

Instead we place our faith and trust in our ability, our power, our possessions. We live as if there will be no tomorrow. But there *will* be a tomorrow, brighter than anything we can imagine today. The great pie in the sky actually exists! To the extent that we are willing to let go of our fears and trust the Savior with every aspect of our lives, to that same extent we can experience a little of the wonder and glory that will someday be fully ours.

Gusto living can begin today for those who live with nothing to lose.

---

1. Larry Crabb, *Inside Out* (Colorado Springs: Navpress, 1988), ch. 5.

Chapter 12

THINGS AND STUFF

He who dies with the most toys . . .
still dies.

Many years ago comedian George Carlin had a hilarious routine about *stuff*. The first time I heard it, I laughed until I couldn't breathe. Carlin's body language, voice inflections, and timing were perfect. I've heard hundreds of comedy routines through the years, but only a few of them stick. This one stayed in my mind not because it was so funny but because it was based on such solid truth: we waste a good portion of our lives accumulating, storing, and protecting *stuff*. Carlin masterfully portrayed the deficiencies of materialism, and I've adapted the next few paragraphs from his comments.

Children fare pretty well until we give them stuff. From that time forward, they begin to spend enormous amounts of time and energy managing and protecting their stuff. *Mine* is one of the first words many children utter. When they are very young, we build them a little box designed specifically to store their stuff. They guard that box like a mother bear defends her cubs. I remember my sister pushing me down a flight of stairs because I touched her stuff.

Later in life, we get our own room. Why do we need our own room? Millions of people around the world grow up perfectly happily without their own room. There's no reason to have our own room, except that it's a bigger place to keep our stuff. This is our territory. All of the stuff in our room is *our stuff!* Except for the stuff we borrowed from brothers or sisters without asking.

When we grow to be adults, we build big toy boxes. We call them houses. The house contains all the stuff that an adult has accumulated. We are just as protective of the stuff in our house as we were the stuff in our toy box. Soon we build a garage next to the house, because all our stuff will no longer fit in the house. I know, a garage is supposed to be a place to store your car. But if you are like me, your car sits outside much of the time, because the garage is filled with stuff.

Speaking of cars—they have become much more than a mode of transportation. They are a status symbol. A big, shiny car is a sure indication to the neighbors that the owner must have a ton of other stuff somewhere. And who hasn't spent a Saturday afternoon cleaning even more stuff out of a car?

Sometimes we go away and leave the bulk of our stuff behind for short periods of time. Even then we pack baggage so we can take some of our stuff with us. Finally, at the end of life, we bequeath our stuff to our kids, forcing them to work hard so that they will have enough stuff for collateral to get a loan to build a place to store the stuff we left them.

That picture is both funny and tragic—because it's true. We focus our energy, time, and resources on buying and protecting stuff, in spite of the fact that when we die, every one of us will leave our stuff behind. We miss out on so much of life because we are protecting the stuff we are afraid to lose.

Our material belongings become our identity, our security, our hope—and our god. We evaluate opportunities and plan our future not in order to serve God as best we can but rather to best enable ourselves to accumulate more stuff and to hang on to the stuff we've already got. True gusto living will never come to anyone who isn't willing to risk their stuff for the better life that God has in mind for us. He who dies with the most toys ... still dies. God is so much bigger than the little gods we choose to serve. As a child, I learned a little poem that best expresses the concept of what really counts in life:

Only one life,
'twill soon be past.
Only what's done
for Christ will last.

A Challenge to Faith

A man was hiking through a mountainous area one day when he came to the top of a high, rocky cliff from which he could see for many miles. It was a clear day, and he stood at the edge of the cliff for a while, resting from his hike and enjoying the view. Suddenly the loose ground at the edge of the cliff gave way beneath his feet, and he plummeted over the edge!

Fortunately, as he fell he was able to grab a branch of a small, scrubby tree growing out of the side of the cliff. But when he looked up, he realized that there was no way for him to climb back up.

He knew he couldn't hang that way for long. He needed help. And even though he'd seen no one else at the top, he yelled, "Help! Somebody help me, please!"

Imagine his surprise when a deep, echoing voice answered from high above him, "I will help you."

But when the man looked up, he saw no one.

"Where are you?" he shouted.

The voice came back, "I am God, and I will help you."

"Throw me down a rope," the man yelled.

"I don't have a rope," God replied.

"If you don't have a rope, how can you help me?" the man cried in frustration.

"Do you trust me?" God asked in his booming voice.

What choice do I have? the man thought, but he called back, "Yes, I trust you!"

"Do you really trust me?" God asked again.

"Yes, I really trust you—but please hurry, I'm losing my grip!"

"If you really trust me," God said, "let go of the branch."

The man was silent for a moment, and then he yelled out, "Is there anybody *else* up there?"[1]

A funny joke—but its humor reflects the tragic way we often live. God is our only hope—our only hope of salvation, our only hope of fulfillment, our only hope for gusto living. Yet it seems we will try anything and everything before we are willing to let go of the *stuff* that is draining our lives of vitality and abundance and allow God to show us some *real* living. We hang on to the scrubby little branches of life and miss out on discovering God's unfailing faithfulness.

The True Cost of Stuff

A missionary told this story: The natives in the country he was living in hunted monkeys for food. But the monkeys were so timid, so terrified of humans, that hunting the monkeys with primitive bows, arrows, and spears was out of the question. The natives couldn't get close enough for a shot.

But these natives found a unique way to trap the monkeys. The natives would drill a hole in one end of a coconut and pour out the milk. Then they would put a nut or some other morsel inside the coconut and tie the coconut to a tree. Despite their fear of the smell of people, the monkeys could smell that morsel of food, and they couldn't resist. A monkey would approach the coconut, stick his hand through the hole, and grasp the nut. But the hole had been purposely drilled just big enough so that the monkey could get his hand *in*—but once his fist was wrapped around the morsel, he couldn't get his hand *out* without first dropping the morsel. His closed fist wouldn't fit through the hole. So intent was the monkey on keeping what was in his hand that he would pull and yank until his wrist was raw and bleeding. But still he would refuse to let go of the nut. When the natives came with clubs and began to beat the monkey, he would still refuse to let go. Only when death relaxed his little hand was the monkey free from this trap. But by then it was too late.

If the *stuff* of life—the morsel in the coconut that we hold so tightly—were the secret to happiness, then we would be able to observe that truth all around us in everyday life. The more things people would have, the happier and more fulfilled they would be. Why, then, is the reverse so often true?

Comedian Freddy Prinze was at the height of his career when he put a gun to his head and pulled the trigger. A baffled world tried to figure out why anyone riding such a wave of success would take his own life. Perhaps a statement that Prinze made shortly before his death tells us part of the answer. Stepping from the stage one night after a very successful performance, he said, "I can't hear them laughing anymore." He couldn't? There was nothing wrong with his hearing, and his audiences were laughing harder than ever. Maybe what he was really saying was, *Their laughter no longer sustains me.* Even so, Prinze had spent so many years scratching to gain his position as a respected television personality that he refused to give it up. It was his security and the foundation of his sense of worth. The last time I saw him, he was still very unhappy—and still desperately clutching the one thing that kept him trapped.

For each of us, the morsel in the trap may be different. It may be a job, a car, a position, an income, even a destructive relationship. But for each of us, the price of hanging on to the morsel is the same. It costs us our *freedom,* our ability to be everything God wants us to be. This short poem illustrates that cost:

> Of all sad words
> Of tongue or pen,
> The saddest are these:
> *It might have been.*

If only we had listened to the gentle call of a Savior who wanted only the best for us. But like that monkey, often we refuse to release our *stuff,* our morsel, until it is too late.

Morsel hoarding has a specific name in the Bible. It is called *idolatry.* It doesn't matter whether your idol is a little carved statue sitting in a shrine built in a corner of your home or a beautiful Mercedes Benz sitting in the garage. If it is more important than God, if it is standing in the way of what he wants for your life—then it needs to go.

The writer of Hebrews gave instructions for those who wanted to persevere in their faith to the end. He said, "Throw off *everything that hinders* and the sin that so easily entangles, and let us run with perseverance the race marked out for us" (Hebrews 12:1, emphasis added). Notice that in that verse these things that hinder are listed separately from other sin. That may be because these *things,* in and of themselves, may not be sinful—they become sin when they hinder us in the race that God has chosen for us.

The essence of faith is letting go of all these things and letting God have a free hand to give us his best. Until we are willing to live with nothing to lose, we will never experience his full power and intention for our lives. We will never experience real living.

Let's Do It Again

One day when my daughter Traci was two and a half years old, I found her standing at the edge of the landing at the top of the stairs, looking down as though she might jump. She looked down at me with an odd, uneasy smile and said, "When I look down, it makes my rear feel funny."

I opened my mouth to demand that she get down from there before she hurt herself, but then I had an idea: I would test how much she trusted me. I stood below where she was teetering on the edge. "Jump!" I said. "I'll catch you."

She inched toward the edge, took a deep breath, and then scrambled back to safety. She did the same thing several more times, trying to work up the courage to jump. Each time, I reassured her that I would never let her fall; and each time, she would lean out a little bit farther before cringing back. Finally, with a desperate groan, she leaned out so far that she could not turn back. With little arms flailing and a scream tearing from her throat, she fell—and I caught her, just as I had promised.

Suddenly she realized she was safe. A smile wiped all the fear from her face, and she yelled, "Let's do it again!"

This is the kind of trust that God wants us to have in him. He doesn't expect us to scream, "Go for it!" and leap blindly into thin air. He just wants us to lean on him until we can't turn back. That can be frightening, but the rewards will make us want to do it again and again.

Instead we want to see a list of possible outcomes and calculate their probability before we let go of anything. But God doesn't promise to reveal every little turn the future will take. If he did, we would be so frightened that we would destroy the blueprint as we sprinted toward some other option. What God *does* promise is to give us grace for each moment.

He doesn't ask you to immediately let go of all the false securities you have accumulated and to forget about them for the rest of your life. He just asks you to let go of the thing his Spirit brings to mind this moment. When the other moments come, he will provide the strength to trust him. His response to our concerns and reluctance is: "Therefore do not worry about tomorrow, for tomorrow will worry about itself. Each day has enough trouble of its own" (Matthew 6:34).

God's instruction is specific:

> Do not store up for yourselves treasures on earth, where moth and rust destroy, and where thieves break in and steal. But store up for yourselves treasures in heaven, where moth and rust do not destroy, and where thieves do not break in and steal. (Matthew 6:19–20)

Our Creator knows that we are incapable of splitting our loyalties. We cannot share our hearts with more than one God.

> For where your treasure is, there your heart will be also. . . . No one can serve two masters. Either he will hate the one and love the other, or he will be devoted to the one and despise the other. You cannot serve both God and Money. (Matthew 6:21, 24)

He also knows that only he is capable of meeting even our most basic of needs. He doesn't want us to miss today's blessing because we are clinging to some worthless morsel, worried about how we will survive tomorrow.

> So do not worry, saying, "What shall we eat?" or "What shall we drink?" or "What shall we wear?" For the pagans run after all these things, and your heavenly Father knows that you need them. But seek first his kingdom and his righteousness, and all these things will be given to you as well. (Matthew 6:31–33)

Someone once asked, "How much faith does it take to swim across a swimming pool?" A little boy answered, "Just enough to let go of the edge." He was right. Like my daughter on the stairs, often we listen to the tense feelings in our rears more than we do the promises of God. We are desperately afraid to live with nothing to lose. As a result, we miss out on experiencing the trusting arms of Christ. Remember the hiker who wouldn't let go of the branch? What are the branches *you* cling to that keep you from discovering that God can be trusted—that keep you from experiencing abundant living?

Friends?

A job?

A car?

A position of prestige?

A nest egg?

A hobby?

A habit?

A lifestyle?

Or is it something else entirely?

Don't expect to feel brave as you let go of some of your handholds of security. At first you may kick and scream, just as my daughter did. God doesn't promise that following him will be painless or easy, but he does promise to be there to catch you when you need him. And he promises that trusting him will bring more joy, fulfillment, and gusto to your life than all the morsels, bushes, and swimming pool edges put together.

---

1. Ken Davis and Dave Lambert, *Jumper Fables* (Grand Rapids: Zondervan, 1994), 117.

Chapter 13

THE SECRET

There are two kinds of people in the world: Givers and takers. The takers eat better.

The givers sleep better.

There is a well-kept secret that can put men and women on the track to gusto living. Actually, it's no secret at all—but it's a concept so foreign to our society that few people even consider it an option. This is the secret:

Life's greatest fulfillment comes from serving.

Ironic, isn't it? The meaning and purpose we seek in life comes from *giving* what we are and what we have rather than living to *get* everything we can. Just as we derive meaning and value from being loved by our Creator, we in turn were designed to love those around us and by doing so draw them to him. That love is more than just a warm, gooey feeling. It is expressed in action, and that action is called service.

Service, believe it or not, is the way we operate best—the way we were *designed* to operate. In our relationship with God and with our fellow man, a spirit of sacrifice and compassion leads to abundant life. Jesus himself spoke of this truth many times throughout Scripture. When the disciples were arguing about who among them was the greatest, "Jesus called the

Twelve and said, 'If anyone wants to be first, he must be the very last, and the servant of all'" (Mark 9:35).

If the focus of life is to accumulate wealth, power, and prestige, then life is truly in vain, because in the end, we gain nothing. After the death of John D. Rockefeller, a man asked his accountant, "How much did he leave?" The accountant replied, "He left everything."

It makes little sense to waste life accumulating what you cannot keep. If you were told today that you had only a few days to live, it's not likely that you would frantically try to accumulate more *stuff* in the short time available. Relatively speaking, we *do* have only a few days to live. Yet far too many of us waste those precious moments in pursuit of things that can never satisfy.

It's tempting to respond to that dilemma, as many throughout history have, by saying, "So what? If I can't take it with me, then I might as well enjoy as much of it as I can while I'm here. I'll eat, drink, and be merry, for tomorrow I'll die anyway." That philosophy leads to a foolish waste of your life in seeking empty pleasures. If you're searching for gusto living—maximum living—you won't find it there. True fulfillment in life comes not from taking everything you can get but from giving whatever you have.

It's obvious that, in our culture, many of us have made the foolish choice to seek pleasure rather than meaning in life. Why, if the life of the self-centered pleasure-seeker is so empty, don't we change our lifestyles and begin living to serve others? There are two basic reasons. First, our thinking has been short-circuited by the mistaken ideas of servanthood that are so prevalent in our society. And second, we've been disconnected from the power source that would enable us to live the difficult life of a servant.

Our Thinking Has Been Short-Circuited

We believe that only the weak serve. The thought of living to serve anyone but ourselves is almost repulsive. This view was expressed in caustic terms by the philosopher Friedrich Nietzsche. Because of Christ's emphasis on servanthood, Nietzsche characterized Christianity as "having a slave morality, making man a sublime abortion."[1]

In our culture, servants are perceived as lower-class, less-capable people. Serving others is considered undignified. Why be the servant when you can be the master? Why dedicate yourself to the welfare of others when you can be watching out for number one? Why lose your life in the will of the heavenly Father when you can do what you please? The movers and shakers in our world don't serve—they are served by others. "Important" people don't concern themselves with meeting the needs of others—unless there is a profit in it.

But the Bible tells a different story. According to Scripture, the world's view of power and servanthood is a misconception. The real truth is this: servanthood is not a sign of weakness; it is a sign of great inner strength. Only those who are secure in the true source of their power and strength are capable of servanthood, because their personal worth is not measured by superficial things. They have no facade to maintain. They have nothing to lose by serving. They serve because they are free to do so. They serve because they want to.

People who depend on the external symbols of worth and power, on the other hand, are rendered incapable of serving. On the outside, they display the appearance of confidence, but beneath the facade there is only an empty husk of real life, a husk devoid of fulfillment and filled with insecurity and self-doubt. They cannot afford vulnerability or caring—that would damage their image. Their work, their toys, their positions, are the only security they have. Take those symbols away, and the people who depend on them would crumble emotionally and physically. Here's the pity: From that position of wealth, power, and authority, they could—if they weren't so self-absorbed—reach out to do great good for those who are powerless.

The loving father of a newborn baby doesn't demonstrate his authority by dashing his baby to the floor. Instead he holds the child with great tenderness—willing, if need be, to sacrifice his own life to save the life of his child. He lives to serve the defenseless baby he helped bring into the world.

Likewise, those who are advocates for the poor or have dedicated their lives to serving others live with much more passion and motivation than those who live just to serve themselves. Mother Teresa, who sacrifices all that she is and all that she has for those she serves, exudes a vitality and a passion for life that transcend her age, her physical stature, and her social position. In worldly terms, she is powerless. She spends her life amid the squalor of impoverished people, scrubbing the filth from babies who have little or no chance of survival. Yet this woman commands the attention of the world's leaders. We stand in awe as she rebukes presidents and proclaims unpopular truth on platforms that will never be granted to you or me. The jaded, materialistic students of an Ivy League school recently responded to her call for compassion with a standing ovation. These are the same students who yawn at the pontifications of powerful political figures. There is more gusto in her frail body than in all the well-tanned bodies at a hundred cocktail parties in the power circles of Washington.

Christ had the power and authority to destroy the human race had he chosen to do so. Because of our sin, he would have been justified in making that choice. Yet without hesitation, he chose instead to serve. He freely gave up his place at the right hand of the Father, taking on the role of a servant, so that he could free us. His example becomes the model for power, authority, and servanthood—a model that we, as his followers, must recognize.

If we agree, then, that only the truly powerful are free to serve, then why is that truth so alien to the modern mind—even the modern mind of the Christian? The answer is that we've been unplugged.

Somebody Pulled the Plug

We have lost our ability to serve, or even to comprehend a life of service, because we have been disconnected from the power source that would enable us to do so. Like an unplugged refrigerator, we take up space but can't keep things fresh.

Sin has had a devastating impact on the environment and on the moral tenor of the world, but some of its greatest damage has been to our ability to love God and to serve each other. Satan must throw back his head and laugh as we indulge ourselves in pleasure and in the accumulation of *stuff* and think we are getting life's best. He laughs because he knows we are missing out on the true joy that life offers. A human life turned inward has a very limited view. That same life turned outward has limitless potential. Unfortunately, unless we are confident in our relationship with God, we will look to the false symbols of the world for our emotional and personal survival. We will take as much as possible, giving only what is necessary. You'll find this egocentric lifestyle in all levels of society and among all races and creeds. It is not just a malady of the rich and famous. You can find the same attitudes in ghettos and poverty-stricken, backcountry bayous. It often worms its way into my life. Every day I fight the temptation (not always successfully) to live for myself and forget servanthood.

Only by connecting with the real source of our power and worth will we find the strength to serve. What will give us the confidence to serve without fear? Only the truth. And where can we find that truth?

Three Facts That Free Us to Serve

One of the most poignant stories in the life of Christ reveals that truth—the truth that frees us to be successful servants. The gospel of John records the day in history that the King of Kings demonstrated his servanthood in a way that shocked even his disciples. At a dinner with his respected friends, Christ removed his outer garments, put on an apron, and washed the disciples' feet. This task was normally considered to be below the dignity of a respectable Jewish man. Washing guests' feet was clearly unpleasant, and that's why it was the duty of the lowest servant of the household.[2]

We can imagine a slave or servant doing such a thing. But a king? Wouldn't performing such a humble task bring humiliation and embarrassment to someone mighty enough to hold the power of the universe in his hands? *Why* would he use those hands to wash the filth of the road from the feet of these men? Why didn't he hire someone else to do this demeaning task?

The English historian Lord Acton once said, "Power tends to corrupt, and absolute power corrupts absolutely." The more power a person has, the more that person tends to wield the power to his own advantage. Yet Christ, who had absolute power, chose to serve in the most humble of ways. What source of strength gave him the ability to do this? Why didn't he feel denigrated? Hidden in this fascinating story are the answers to those questions—and the secret that can release us to serve others.

> It was just before the Passover Feast. Jesus knew that the time had come for him to leave this world and go to the Father. Having loved his own who were in the world, he now *showed them the full extent of his love.* (John 13:1, emphasis added)

Don't let the impact of those last few words slip by. What Jesus was about to do was not a casual demonstration of emotion or merely an object lesson in humility. The Bible says that this was a demonstration of the *full extent of his love*! He did not demonstrate his love with a soppy speech or an expensive gift.

Instead he demonstrated his love in humble service to those he loved—and by so doing created an example they would never forget.

> The evening meal was being served, and the devil had already prompted Judas Iscariot, son of Simon, to betray Jesus. Jesus knew that the Father had put all things under his power, and that he had come from God and was returning to God; *so* he got up from the meal, took off his outer clothing, and wrapped a towel around his waist. After that, he poured water into a basin and began to wash his disciples' feet, drying them with the towel that was wrapped around him. (John 13:2–5, emphasis added)

Imagine visiting a government dignitary and enjoying the final course of a wonderful meal. As you sit back to relax, your host puts on a servant's clothes, kneels in front of you, and begins to wash your feet. You would be just as uncomfortable and bewildered as the disciples were. Peter was so upset that he refused to let Jesus wash his feet.

> "No," said Peter, "you shall never wash my feet." Jesus answered, "Unless I wash you, you have no part with me."[3] (John 13:8)

How could someone with such power and prestige humble himself so totally? And yet despite the humbling nature of his action, Christ does not, in this passage of Scripture, seem humiliated or embarrassed. Why is that? Where did he find the inner strength to set aside his rightful authority and become a mere servant? The answer is found in verses 3 and 4:

> Jesus knew that the Father had put all things under his power, and that he had come from God and was returning to God; so he got up from the meal, took off his outer clothing, and wrapped a towel around his waist. After that, he poured water into a basin and began to wash his disciples' feet. (John 13:3–5)

These verses indicate that Jesus was aware and confident of three facts:

He knew that the Father had put all things under his power.
He knew that he had come from God.
He knew that he was going back to God.

His awareness of these three things gave him the power to serve. The first word in verse 4 is *so*, indicating that his demonstration of service in verses 4 and 5 was motivated by what had just been disclosed in verse 3. If I was to say, "I love my daughter. I am lonesome for her because she went away to college, and I want to see her again—so I'm flying out to visit her," you would have no doubt about why I was going. It's because I love her and I want to see her. Likewise, Jesus washed the feet of his friends because of those three truths.

The answer to the question, How could he do such a thing? is clear: because he had the authority and power to do it. No task was so humiliating, no service so demeaning, that it could change the truth. No task could diminish his power, dim the glory of his heritage, or threaten the security of his future.

Washing the disciples' feet would not change Christ's status. He had created the earth, and all the earth was still under his power, where God the Father had placed it. Even as he rubbed the dirty soles (souls?) of the first man in line, Jesus was aware that he had come from God. That made his touch neither tentative nor squeamish but instead firm and gentle. As he dried the last foot, with the odor of sweat and road filth still lingering in the air, he knew that soon he would be returning to God. His humble act did not change these truths. Rather it was precisely these truths that freed him to perform this humble act. Jesus knew the truth—even if those around him did not—about his relationship to his Father, and he knew his purpose on earth. Jesus had nothing to prove and nothing to hide. Therefore he had nothing to lose. If his own image and position had been in doubt, Jesus would have demanded that the disciples wash *his* feet.

The most exciting news is this: The same three facts that gave Jesus the confidence to serve are true of us as well—and can give us that same confidence. First, the same Christ who has been given power over the entire universe is our source of strength. Our power does not come from the positions we hold, the status we achieve, or any other source originating within ourselves. Our power is in him (Acts 1:8). That source of power doesn't change, regardless of our earthly position. We can't lose face with God. No task can change the fact that we are children of *the* King. We are free to wipe the vomit from the sick and hold the hopeless in our arms. We are free to do these things because he is the source of our power.

Second, we too came from God (Ephesians 3:14–15; Colossians 1:16). What greater authority could we claim? If we are truly his creation and his children, then passing out blankets or ministering to men and women who have committed crimes becomes not a threat to our security but rather an honor. The false symbols of security and status given so much weight by our culture have no relevance at all to a people who came from God—and we are that people.

Third, we are going to return to God (Colossians 3:4). Most people find servanthood repulsive because they view their lives as the proving ground of their worth, as we discussed in part 1 of this book. Those who view life in that way will never have the strength to truly serve others. But those who know that they are serving at the command of the King of the universe, who understand that they have been created, loved, and redeemed by the living God, and who believe that they will return to that God to experience love and glory beyond imagination—those people are free to serve without fear of affecting their image. They know that their image was established before the beginning of time and sealed on a cross. Their future was guaranteed by an empty grave. They live in his power, and they can serve without fear.

So What?

Even granted that all of this is true, it has practical value only if God does indeed expect us to serve others. Let's return to the footwashing incident.

> "Do you understand what I have done for you?" he asked them. "You call me 'Teacher' and 'Lord,' and rightly so, for that is what I am. Now that I, your Lord and Teacher, have washed your feet, you also should wash one another's feet. I have set you an example that you should do as I have done for you." (John 13:12–15)

What did Christ mean by this? I doubt that he intended for us to set up footwashing booths at restaurants, like the car washes we see beside gas stations. The true challenge goes far beyond an occasional foot bath. *How* far?

> Your attitude should be the same as that of Christ Jesus: Who, being in very nature God, did not consider equality with God something to be grasped, but made himself nothing, taking the very nature of a servant, being made in human likeness. And being found in appearance as a man, he humbled himself and became obedient to death—even death on a cross! Therefore God exalted him to the highest place and gave him the name that is above every name. (Philippians 2:5–9)

What A Wonderful World It Would Be

I doubt that there is a more difficult concept to grasp and live out than loving servanthood. Yet I'm also convinced that there is none more important. The world is starved for a demonstration of love like this. Think of how such service would transform our neighborhoods. Think of how it would transform our government. The welfare system would disappear for lack of business as men and women reached out to help each other rather than expecting the government to do it. Communities would provide services that helped the elderly, the young, and the less fortunate.

Yet we live in a world that tenaciously clings to values that are just the opposite of selfless servanthood. If there ever was a "Me Generation," this is it. Personal rights are flaunted at the expense of everyone else. Selfishness, greed, and assertiveness are *valued* attributes, since they help one to "get ahead." Children are neglected so that parents can be "self-fulfilled." Marriages are abandoned so that the partners can "find" themselves. Winning is pursued at any cost, in everything from sports to business to entertainment. The result: society is falling apart at the seams. What a breath of fresh air, what a different culture it would be, if people genuinely began to care for each other.

If just the body of Christ would begin to consistently live in this way, the church would be looked at in a whole new light by the secular world. Loving service to each other is the greatest demonstration we can make of our love for Christ. Just before he was to be crucified, Jesus sat with his disciples and explained that where he was going, they would not be able to follow—but that he had something of extreme importance to tell them. Those words were among the last he spoke before going to the cross. We must not minimize their significance:

> "A new command I give you: Love one another. As I have loved you, so you must love one another. All men will know that you are my disciples, if you love one another." (John 13:34–35)

If Jesus had been just a "good ol' boy" who gave expensive gifts to his friends and always had an encouraging word for folks, then following that command would be relatively simple. But he expressed his love for us in the most humble and awesome way possible, in an act of love that made the footwashing incident shrink into relative insignificance. He suffered—for the sake of men and women who had sinned against him—the death of a common criminal. He willingly subjected himself to a humiliating death on the cross so that you and I could live.

He said that we, his followers, are to love each other with the same intense, unconditional love. He said that our love for each other would alert the world to the fact that we are his followers. It's not our regular attendance at church, not our successful business, not our avoidance of the Nine Nasties—it is our love that makes the world sit up and take notice.

What Does Service Have to Do with Gusto Living?

Only those who are free to live with nothing to prove, nothing to hide, and nothing to lose can even come close to tasting the sweetness that a life of service brings. But this truth, even though it's relatively easy to talk about (or even to write about), is so very difficult to act upon. Breaking free from the hold of this world's values and actually living a life of service is the real test of faith. Progress can be agonizingly slow, but each tiny step brings us closer to what God wants us to be. Only in the last few years have I been able to even consider making such an effort. I still cling to so many of the superficial things in life.

But if we see earthly things as the ultimate goal of our lives, we will never live to our fullest potential, never find the gusto we seek. Paul said it even better: "Set your minds on things above, not on earthly things" (Colossians 3:2). Full-potential living goes beyond the temporal. It draws from the limitless power of God (Colossians 3:1–2). Around the world, there are godly men and women who serve others and demonstrate in that life of service the truth and effectiveness of God's power. In those lives, boldness replaces fear, confidence replaces timidity, humility replaces pride, love replaces lust (the desire to possess), and compassion replaces loathing. In the chapter to follow, we'll look at some of those lives.

If we can find the courage to trust God to enable us to live lives of service, not only will we begin to move closer to our fullest potential but our families, friends, and business associates

will look at us in a different light. They may not understand our
behavior—they may, in fact, wonder whether we have lost touch
with reality—but somewhere deep in their souls, they will know
who is behind this inexplicable behavior. Somehow they will
know that we follow him.

Jesus, the one who claimed the greatest victory of all time,
did so by becoming a servant. He wants to share that victory with
you.

> "The man who loves his life will lose it, while the man who
> hates his life in this world will keep it for eternal life. Whoever
> serves me must follow me; and where I am, my servant also
> will be. My Father will honor the one who serves me." (John
> 12:25–26)

---

1. Friedrich Nietzsche, *Beyond Good and Evil*, trans. R. J. Holingdale (New
   York: Penguin, 1972), 71, 175.
2. *The Zondervan Pictorial Bible Dictionary* (Grand Rapids: Zondervan,
   1967), 288.
3. R. V. G. Tasker points out that this is not simply "a striking example of the
   nobility of serving others." Instead in "this sacramental action Jesus is
   illustrating the cleansing power of his death" (R. V. G. Tasker, *The Gospel
   According To St. John,* Tyndale New Testament Commentary Series
   [Grand Rapids: Eerdmans, 1977], 154–55).

Chapter 14

A FEW WHO DARED

He is no fool who gives what he
cannot keep to gain what he cannot
lose.

—Jim Elliot

A Wake-up Call—to Life

While visiting Texas in the early eighties, I met many people who had lost everything because of a fall in oil prices. Overnight, men and women who had controlled vast empires of wealth found themselves penniless. Jim was one of those men. I had dinner at his home one evening. Amazingly, when Jim and his family prayed, they praised God for the financial fall they had experienced! It wasn't the kind of bogus, mumbo-jumbo prayer that people say to impress others with their spirituality, nor was it the kind of meaningless prayer that people sometimes say because they know they're supposed to. These people *meant* it. Their prayer was a sincere thank-you to God for what they called the "wake-up call" in their lives.

After dinner I asked Jim and his wife how they could thank God for what seemed like such a disaster. "It was only when almost everything I valued in life—my possessions, my status, my bank account, my company—was forcibly taken from me,"

Jim explained, "that the scales fell from my eyes, allowing me to see what was really important. The truth was, I didn't control my wealth—it controlled me."

"When OPEC took our fortune," his wife added, "God gave me back my husband, and the kids back their father."

Things would never be the same for Jim and his family. He had rediscovered the road to maximum living. He had not found maximum living in the oil field, nor had he found it in the corporate boardroom. But all that time, it had been as close as God's voice. When things finally quieted down enough for Jim to hear that voice, he responded to it, and today he is a different person.

Today Jim is building his company back up again, but not at the expense of his family or his walk with Christ. Today he acknowledges that everything he has belongs to God. His relationships—with God and with his family—take precedence over what he owns. He runs his business with integrity and excellence and shares his success with those who are less fortunate. Most important of all, he is willing to give it all up in an instant if God should require that of him. Jim is getting more out of life than ever before—because he lives with nothing to lose.

Gusto Living for Gutsy People

One of the most exciting and vibrant men I have ever met is Don Richardson, author of the best-selling book *Peace Child*. God gave Don a great mind, a taste for adventure, and a heart for service—a pretty powerful combination. His intelligence and capabilities opened the door for him to write his own ticket in the world. He could have been a professor at a prestigious university and lived a comfortable life, with social respect and financial security. His creative ability and people skills would have made it possible for him to sit at the helm of any major corporate enterprise. I saw his intelligence in action one night when he beat me at chess while discussing some abstract philosophical

point with a friend. I think he could have beat me while simul-
taneously computing his income tax and writing a book.

Instead of choosing one of those lucrative occupations and
playing it safe, Don chose to follow the urging of God's Spirit
calling him to service to others. Instead of beginning his married
life by carrying his wife over the threshold of a comfortable sub-
urban home, Don took his bride to New Guinea, where they
would spend the prime years of their lives as missionaries to the
Sawi people. Shortly after their first child was born, Don stepped
out of a primitive canoe one day and stood surrounded by head-
hunting cannibals on the banks of a remote jungle river:

> Down the last stretch, Carol and I peered ahead through
> legs and paddles, trying to catch a first glimpse of our home
> and of . . . ? We were not prepared for what we saw! About two
> hundred armed warriors thronged the shore, looming into
> stark silhouette against a red-gold horizon. Feathers bristled
> from their hair and fluttered from their spears. Further back,
> and closer to the small cut-pole house John and I had com-
> pleted three days earlier, an equal number of women and
> small children watched us, exclaiming in hushed tones over
> our strange appearance.
>
> Our paddlers grew silent as we glided in and struck shore
> at the feet of the armed multitude.[1]

As Don and his family stood on the shore, surrounded by
people known to be hostile and violent, his mind was filled with
momentary doubt. Even though it was too late to turn back, he
grappled one last time with the question, *Why am I here?* In the
midst of unfamiliar chaos and danger and with his wife and baby
by his side, Don, in silent communication with God, put the
question to rest once and for all:

> It was a question I had often fielded from the lips of unbe-
> lievers. Now my Lord was asking it, and there was no escape
> from the question. The eyes of every Sawi dancer seemed to
> ask it. Their voices seemed to chant it, their drums to echo
> it. . . .

I reviewed answers I had used in the past, discarding
them one by one. Secondary, incidental reasons no longer
mattered. Nor could ulterior ambitions endure the four-
dimensional reality our task had now assumed.

The descent to new bedrock took a few minutes. Then I
breathed my answer:

"Lord Jesus, it is for You we stand here, immersed not in
water but in Sawi humanity. This is our baptism into the work
You anticipated for us before creation. Keep us faithful.
Empower us with Your Spirit.

"May Your will be done among these people, as it is in
heaven. And if any good comes to them through us, the honor
is Yours!"

And He replied, "The peace of God, which passes all
understanding, shall garrison your hearts and minds through
Christ."

It was all right now. Our relationship was renewed. I
could feel a fresh spring welling up inside.[2]

At that moment, Don and his family had none of the securities that you and I hold so tightly. His neighbors were warring
tribes who took pride in treachery and deceit. The greatest tri-
umph of these tribes was to win the trust of an enemy and then,
when the enemy least expected it, to murder them and eat their
flesh. Don's difficult task was to bring the good news of Christ to
a people who couldn't understand peace. The cycles of treachery
and violence were destroying their culture. The Sawi honored
those who were good at betrayal. When Don told them the story
of the crucifixion, they chose Judas as their hero.

Why would such a talented and gifted man begin his married
life by exposing his family to such danger? Why should he waste
his talents on such ignorant, treacherous people? In *Peace Child,*
it is clear that Don had no such doubts:

> With earnest longing we pleaded with God that the mes-
> sage of redemption in Christ might quickly break through all
> barriers, satanic or cultural, and spread this blessed contagion

of joy to those strange, fearful men we had encountered that morning on the Kronkel River. How long it would take, I could not even guess. I only knew that my life would not be complete until it happened![3]

God called Don Richardson to a dark land and gave him a life brighter and more full of excitement than most people would ever hope to experience. Don's gifts and talents were used to the full. His inquisitive and analytical mind was put to work solving a mystery as thrilling as that found in any novel. After years of frustration spent watching the tribes murder and betray each other, Don discovered the key to opening their hearts. The secret lay within the elements of their own culture.

Even in that dark society where murder and deceit were valued, he discovered a parallel to the gospel that finally enabled him to get a message of God's love through. And when they were finally able to hear the gospel, the transformation in the lives of those natives who trusted Christ is nothing short of miraculous.

Although he is now living in the United States, Don's life is no less dynamic. The gifts that God has given him are being channeled in new and powerful directions. The key is this: He is using those gifts to serve God and others.

I first heard Don's story when he told it to a group of successful men and women on a cruise ship. As he spoke, I looked around the room and saw many eyes filled with tears. (I was looking to see whether mine were the only ones.) I saw wealthy, socially connected people who were more than just fascinated with his story; they were strongly moved. I doubt that any of us on that ship had some secret desire to live with cannibals or to build a grass hut. Rather we were moved because every one of us would love to find the kind of fire and enthusiasm for life that Don expressed.

I returned to my room after hearing him speak and wept. I had seen an example of a man who lived life to the fullest. I had sat in a front-row seat and observed real gusto living—and it had reminded me of the shortcuts I had taken in my own life. I was suddenly aware of those times I had yielded to the seductive temptation to live with something to prove, something to hide, or something to lose, and I mourned the loss of precious time. I found myself on my knees that night, drawn once again to the Creator, the only one who could guide me to maximum living.

Early in life, Don Richardson had yielded his life to God and followed God's prompting. As a result, his eyes sparkle with delight when he talks of the adventures that God brought to him and his family. There is no regret. Instead there is a sense of accomplishment and a childlike anticipation that God has even more in store. How often do you find people who live with that kind of passion? How often have you felt it yourself? When we allow anything or anyone other than our Creator to direct our lives, we become like blind slaves pulling on the oars of someone else's ship, without the hope of a clear destination, blind to the option of freedom.

It's time to jump into the Lord's arms once again, time to let go of the things that keep you from life, time to say to God, "Here I am. Take me in the direction you intended for my life and use me to the fullest capacity on the journey."

A Guaranteed Victory—No Matter What

It's doubtful that any other person in history has had a more profound influence on proclaiming the good news of Christ than the apostle Paul. This man lived as if he had nothing to lose, and the result was a dynamic life that affected millions of people and the course of history. Once a bigoted hater of Christians, his life was forever changed by an encounter with the risen Christ. When you consider the horrible adversity he faced, you have to wonder how he endured. At least five of the encouraging letters he wrote to the struggling churches of that day (Ephesians, Philippians, Colossians, Philemon, and 2 Timothy), he wrote from prison. The others were written under life-threatening circumstances. Yet because the cause of Christ was worth more than anything else in the world to him, because he lived with nothing to lose, Paul's life made a difference.

You may think Paul was too serious, you may not even agree with some of the things he said, but no one can say he lived a boring life. He was beaten and jailed. He was threatened and hunted. But his enemies couldn't stop him. How can you deter someone who has nothing to lose? Paul himself said it:

> Who will bring any charge against those whom God has chosen?... Who shall separate us from the love of Christ? Shall trouble or hardship or persecution or famine or nakedness or danger or sword? As it is written: "For your sake we face death all day long; we are considered as sheep to be slaughtered." No, in all these things we are more than conquerors through him who loved us. (Romans 8:33–37)

Paul's enemies didn't realize that there was nothing they could do to hurt him. In spite of all the hardship they heaped upon him, he claimed victory. Because Paul knew that the game was already won, he counted it a privilege to suffer for Christ. Punishing Paul for preaching the gospel was like giving him privileges. Even threatening him with death was useless, because he wasn't afraid to lose his life in the pursuit of being everything that God created him to be: "For to me, to live is Christ and to die is gain" (Philippians 1:21). "If we live, we live to the Lord; and if we die, we die to the Lord. So, whether we live or die, we belong to the Lord" (Romans 14:8).

Eventually Paul's enemies succeeded in killing him. They thought they had gotten him out of their hair. But because his work on earth had been directed by the Creator of the universe, it will continue to impact civilization until the end of time. His enemies thought they had done away with him. But in reality, after Paul drew his last breath on earth, he found himself an instant later in the presence of his Creator, Almighty God. Paul lost nothing in that instant, because he had spent his life preparing for it. And even Paul had not realized just how much he was to gain on the other side of death.

It *Is* Contagious

I met Mike O'Hara in the early seventies. Mike's personality was a whole lot different from Paul's. You wouldn't think of Mike as a saint. Mike would have thought Paul was pretty stuffy, and Paul would probably have written a letter to Mike's church, urging them to pray that Mike would be more sober-minded in the Lord. But Paul and Mike had something in common. In the brief time I knew Mike, his life radiated the testimony of one who was living with nothing to lose.

Mike was in his twenties when we first met. I liked him immediately. He was earthy, not always appropriate, and hilariously creative. Mike had a contagious sense of enthusiasm that made it an adventure just to be around him. But he also had something else.

A few years before I met him, Mike had been diagnosed with a very virulent form of cancer. The cancer had finally reached his lungs, and after several operations, the prognosis was not good: the cancer was not responding to treatment. But he was so young, and he had so much potential! You would have expected such news to be like cold water on his exuberant personality. And to be sure, there were times when Mike wept at the prospect of his life being shortened—especially when he considered the effect his death would have on his new bride, to whom he'd been married for less than a year. But mostly Mike exhibited uncommon grace and unexpected joy throughout his ordeal. When he lost his hair because of the chemotherapy treatments, Mike attended a costume party dressed as a bottle of roll-on deodorant. With Mike you never knew what was coming next. His close friends still laugh at the memory of his antics.

Mike was a staff member of Youth for Christ, and throughout his illness he continued to minister to the needs of students.

One day while visiting a school in which he worked, I watched a troubled, sneering young man in the hallway taunt Mike: "What happened to your hair, baldy?"

I wanted to tear this impudent little punk apart, but Mike had a different response. "The problem is," Mike told him as he walked closer, "I'm dying. I've got cancer, and the baldness is from the chemotherapy treatments." (*That* definitely got the student's attention.) Mike then used that opening to communicate to his young antagonist the good news of Christ. At one point, Mike stood toe-to-toe with the boy, prodding him in the chest with his finger, saying, "You don't have to be afraid."

The boy slapped Mike's hand away and, with a curse, spat that he wasn't afraid of anything. Yet his eyes were filled with fear.

"You *are* afraid," Mike continued, emphasizing each word with another poke to the boy's chest. He shared the message of Christ's love with that boy that morning as clearly and compassionately as anyone I have ever heard. I wish I could say that the boy responded. He didn't. I don't know where he is today. I do know that wherever he is, there's a big bruise on his chest—not from Mike's prodding finger but from the powerful truth of Mike's words. You couldn't have looked into the eyes of a man who knew that he had only a few months to live, seen the joy, trust, excitement, and caring that sparkled there, and not remember it forever.

Later that day, Mike and I went to lunch. As much as I enjoyed Mike's company, I was uncomfortable around him because I was so aware of his illness and of the dire prognosis the doctors had given. Mike must have sensed my uneasiness, because shortly after we sat down, he asked me why I was troubled. "You're nervous around me," he said. "Why?"

I could only shrug my shoulders and mumble, "I don't know."

Leaning across the table with his face just inches from mine,

Mike pointed to his bald head and asked with mock concern, "Do you think this is contagious?"

Again I shrugged my shoulders.

I can still see the mischievous twinkle in Mike's eyes as he laughed, leaned back, and rubbed his hands slowly all over his shiny bald head. Then suddenly he leaned forward and rubbed his hands on *my* head. "It *is* contagious!" he said, laughing loudly.

Now everyone in the restaurant was looking in our direction. Still leaning forward, Mike asked, "You're nervous because I'm dying, aren't you?"

Tears welled up in my eyes as I nodded. Yes, it was because he was dying.

"You dummy!" he said, poking me to establish eye contact. I have never forgotten the next words he said. I still see the sincerity on his face as he calmly said, "Ken, we're both dying. The only difference between you and me is that God has let me know *when* I'm going to die." With one more poke of his finger, he leaned closer and winked, whispering, "Ken, we've got nothing to lose."

I was stunned by the simple truth of his statement. Death is inevitable, but it is not the end. Nor is it the worst thing that can happen to us. Those who have placed their faith and trust in the Savior have *nothing to lose*—not even in the face of death.

I wasn't there when Mike died, but I was told he was with his family. Cancer can be so cruel, especially in those final days, and Mike suffered as many others have. Shortly after his last smile, Mike—like Paul—breathed his last breath on earth, and those who loved him wept. But they couldn't see what happened next. In the next moment, Mike saw the One who loved him more than any other. Paul undoubtedly stood not far away—the injuries from his beatings gone, as well as the emotional troubles that had plagued him in his earthly life. Suddenly Mike realized that his pain was gone. His cancer-ridden body had been left behind, and his new body bore the glory of God's original creation—with hair and everything. Mike was free. He was in the presence of a joy that no words could express. If he had ever doubted what was really important, it was settled now, because now he was seeing the eternal evidence that what he had said to me had been right: he had nothing to lose. I'll guarantee he smiled. He knew it wouldn't be long before those he loved would be able to experience the same incredible joy he knew in that moment.[4]

Are we afraid of the consequences of following Christ? Do we miss our opportunity for gusto living because we clutch what we cannot keep at the expense of what can never be lost? After spending a life punctuated by suffering, incarceration, humiliation, and struggle (more than most of us will ever have to bear), Paul said that he was more than a conqueror. He said that even though we are like sheep being led to the slaughter, we too have victory in Christ. Why? How is it possible? The answer is, We have nothing to lose. The love of Christ that sustains us and that can bring us the ultimate joy possible in this life is a love that cannot be taken away. Not by anything. Not even death.

> No, in all these things we are more than conquerors through him who loved us. [This is why:] For I am convinced that neither death nor life, neither angels nor demons, neither the present nor the future, nor any powers, neither height nor depth, nor anything else in all creation, will be able to separate us from the love of God that is in Christ Jesus our Lord. (Romans 8:37–39)

True faith in God does not consist of trusting him to heal or of trusting him to bless or of trusting him to do any other single thing. True faith is trusting him with *everything* because of what he has already done. True faith in God is trusting him— *period*. It is believing that *all* things work together for good— and then, as a result of that belief, living with nothing to lose.

1. Don Richardson, *Peace Child* (Ventura, Calif.: Regal, 1974), 134.
2. Ibid., 139–40.
3. Ibid., 106.
4. The sequence of events that will take place immediately after death and before the resurrection is not fully explained in the Bible. Biblical scholars and theologians can only make educated guesses in their attempts to peer over the horizon of death, and there are many differences and disagreements among them. In my suppositions about Mike's coming into the presence of Christ, I am taking the generally accepted evangelical view, relying on biblical texts such as Luke 23:43 and 2 Corinthians 5:6–8.

Chapter 15

GOOD NEWS!

As the women made their way through the trees of the grove, the persistent mist hung in the air like a horrible memory. Occasionally, uncomfortable words would push back the suffocating silence that had characterized their journey; then the hush would return, as heavy as the mist. They stopped only once, to quietly comfort one of their number who had broken into sobs; then they continued. The closer they got to the grave, the closer they huddled together.

Each one was dreading the anguish that would accompany their task. It had been only three days since he had died. There had been moments of relief during that time, when some other thought had obscured the horrible truth—but only brief moments. Then that truth would come crashing back: Jesus was dead. The vibrancy and joy he had brought to their lives was gone. He would never teach them or laugh or eat with them again. The hope of salvation he had promised was gone, too—seeped away with the blood that had run from his body, down the cross, and into the ground.

They had had such faith in him. Even as he died, they had expected him to miraculously come down from the cross or call the angels of heaven to rescue him. But even that hope and faith had been crushed as the huge stone sealing his tomb had crunched into place.

Now as they anointed the body of Jesus, they would have to relive the whole nightmare. Denial would be impossible. They would touch and see and smell the evidence that he was dead, and with him all hope.

Their feet grew heavy. The tomb was just through the next stand of trees. They stopped, gathering strength from the understanding and sympathy they saw in each other's eyes. Then quickly they hurried around the final outcropping of rock—and in unison they cried out in terror. Their grief was instantly replaced with confusion and fear. They stumbled backward, falling over one another, hiding their eyes from the brightness of the man who stood at the entrance to Jesus' tomb. Even with their eyes closed, they could see his lingering image. One of the women turned to run, but she was stopped by an incredible voice—not a voice of terror, neither loud nor mystical, it was a voice full of confidence and joy, like the voice of a loving father reassuring his family that all is well:

> "Do not be afraid, for I know that you are looking for Jesus, who was crucified." (Matthew 28:5)

Now fear and confusion crowded their minds. Had Jesus' body been desecrated? Had it been stolen? Were they at the right tomb? Would this man kill them?

Once again, the strong, confident voice demanded their attention. "He is not here," the man said. Then, before the question could even form in the women's minds, he continued: "*He is risen!*"

No mist could mute those words. They reverberated through the tomb and burst forth—just as Christ had. They were amplified by the joy that suddenly flooded the hearts of the women as they looked inside and saw only grave clothes where his body had once been. Those words banished the heavy mist, scattered demons, and brought hope to all humankind.

Bernie, the little boy at Bible camp, heard the words: "He is risen!"

The man on death row heard the words: "He is risen!"

The couple who had just lost a child heard: "He is risen!"

The minister who didn't have the strength to go on heard it, too.

The student who was questioning his faith heard it.

I heard it.

The words penetrated creature and creation, filling the earth: *Good news! Good news! He is risen!*

Can you hear it?

Jesus loved you in spite of your sin, leaving you with nothing to prove. He paid in full the penalty you deserved and forgave you of *everything*—leaving you with nothing to hide. He rose from the dead, forever taking the sting of death and ensuring that *nothing* can separate you from his love.

You can live without fear.

You can risk it all.

You can go for the gusto.

You have nothing to lose.

So the women hurried away from the tomb, afraid yet filled with joy, and ran to tell his disciples. (Matthew 28:8)

Good news!

The author would like to thank the following publishers for permission to quote from the following books:

Ronald B. Allen, *The Majesty of Man*. Published by Multnomah books, Questar Publishers; copyright © 1984 by Ronald Allen.

Philip B. Applewhite, *Molecular Gods*. Reprinted by permission of the publisher, Prentice Hall/A Division of Simon & Schuster.

Mona Charen, "Virtue Vanishing from National Character," used by permission of Mona Charen and Creators Syndicate.

Charles Colson and Jack Eckerd, *Why America Doesn't Work*, © 1991. Word Publishing, Dallas, Texas. All rights reserved.

Larry Crabb, *Inside Out*. © 1991. Used by permission of NavPress.

Ken Davis and Dave Lambert, *Jumper Fables*. Copyright © 1994 by Ken Davis and Dave Lambert. Used by permission of Zondervan Publishing House.

Vernard Eller, *The Mad Morality*. Copyright © 1970 by Abingdon Press. Used by permission.

Viktor Frankl, *Man's Search for Meaning*. Copyright © 1959, 1962, 1984, 1992 by Viktor Frankl. Reprinted by permission of Beacon Press.

Garry Friesen and J. Robin Maxson, *Decision Making and the Will of God*. Published by Multnomah books, Questar Publishers; copyright © 1983.

Gordon R. Lewis and Bruce A. Demarest, *Integrative Theology, vol. 2*. Copyright © 1990 by Gordon R. Lewis and Bruce A. Demarest. Used by permission of Zondervan Publishing House.

Audio pages are available for this book
at fine bookstores everywhere.

ZondervanPublishingHouse

How to live with your kids
When you've already lost your mind.
by Ken Davis

Ken Davis turns his humorous wit and wisdom to addressing the issues parents of teenagers struggle with—such as dis-

cipline, communication (or the lack of it), sexuality, and, of course, the drive for independence. But Ken Davis goes beyond these issues to those we too often overlook, including such things as telling our kids we're sorry, installing character in our kids, and more.

Here is a book filled with both humor and hope. Ken Davis offers the encouragement and practical help all parents are looking for.

ISBN 0-310-57631-8

Also available in AUDIO PAGES
ISBN 0-310-57638-5
(2 60-minute cassettes)

Available at fine bookstores everywhere.

📖 Zondervan Publishing House

How to Live With Your Parents
without losing your mind
by Ken Davis

In this book for teenagers, best-selling author and speaker Ken Davis shows teens how they can change their families by making changes in themselves—and in the way they view their

by Ken Davis

parents. Combining biblical principles and his own humorous style, Davis cuts through the complexities of being a teenager and living in a family.

But this book isn't for teens only. Parents will find new understanding of how they make decisions, express their authority, and express their love.

Here is a book dedicated to promoting harmony within the home.

Softcover, 160 pages 0-310-32331-2

Also available in AUDIO PAGES
0-310-32338-X